VALUATION
WORKBOOK

658. '5
COP   1

WILEY FINANCE

Advanced Fixed-Income Valuation Tools, Narasimham Jegadeesh and Bruce Tuckman
Beyond Value at Risk, Kevin Dowd
Buying and Selling Volatility, Kevin B. Connolly
Chaos and Order in the Capital Markets: New View of Cycles, Prices, and Market Volatility, Second Edition, Edgar E. Peters
Corporate Financial Distress and Bankruptcy, Second Edition, Edward I. Altman
Credit Derivatives: A Guide to Instruments and Applications, Janet Tavakoli
Credit Risk Measurement: New Approaches to Value at Risk and Other Paradigms, Anthony Saunders
Currency Derivatives: Pricing Theory, Exotic Options, and Hedging Applications, David F. DeRosa
Damodaran on Valuation: Analysis for Investment and Corporate Finance, Aswath Damodaran
Derivatives Demystified: Using Structured Financial Products, John C. Braddock
Derivatives for Decision-Makers: Strategic Management Issues, George Crawford and Bidyut Sen
Derivatives Handbook: Risk Management and Control, Robert J. Schwartz and Clifford W. Smith, Jr.
Derivatives: The Theory and Practice of Financial Engineering, Paul Wilmott
Dictionary of Financial Engineering, John F. Marshall
Dynamic Hedging: Managing Vanilla and Exotic Options, Nassim Taleb
The Equity-Risk Premium: Long-Run Future of the Stock Market, Bradford Cornell
Financial Statement Analysis: A Practitioner's Guide, Second Edition, Martin S. Fridson
Fixed Income Securities: Tools for Today's Markets, Bruce Tuckman
Fixed-Income Analysis for the Global Financial Market, Giorgio Questa
The Foreign Exchange and Money Markets, Second Edition, Julian Walmsley
Global Trade Financing, Harry M. Venedikian and Gerald A. Warfield
The Handbook of Equity Derivatives, Revised Edition, Jack Francis, William Toy, and J. Gregg Whittaker
The Independent Fiduciary: Investing for Pension Funds and Endowment Funds, Russell L. Olson
Interest-Rate Option Models, Ricardo Rebonato
International M&A, Joint Ventures, and Beyond: Doing the Deal, David J. BenDaniel and Arthur Rosenbloom
Investing in Africa: An Insider's Guide to the Ultimate Emerging Market, Justin Beckett and Michael Sudarkasa
Investment Management, Peter L. Bernstein and Aswath Damodaran
Investment Timing and the Business Cycle, Jon G. Taylor
Investment Valuation, Aswath Damodaran
M&A: A Practical Guide to Doing the Deal, Jeffrey C. Hooke
Managing Credit Risk: The Next Great Financial Challenge, John Caouette, Edward Altman, and Paul Narayanan
Managing Derivative Risks: The Use and Abuse of Leverage, Lilian Chew
Measuring Market Risk with Value at Risk, Pietro Penza and Vipul K. Bansal
New Dimensions in Investor Relations, Bruce Marcus and Sherwood Wallace
New Financial Instruments: Investor's Guide, Julian Walmsley
Option Pricing Models, Les Clewlow and Chris Strickland
Options on Foreign Exchange, Second Edition, David F. DeRosa
Options, Futures, and Exotic Derivatives: Theory, Application & Practice, Eric Briys
Pension Fund Excellence: Creating Value for Stockholders, Keith P. Ambachtsheer and D. Don Ezra
Portfolio Indexing: Theory and Practice, Harold Hutchinson
Pricing Financial Instruments: The Finite Difference Method, Domingo Tavella and Curt Randall
Project Financing: Asset-Based Financial Engineering, John D. Finnerty
Relative Dividend Yield: Common Stock Investing for Income and Appreciation, Second Edition, Anthony E. Spare
Risk Arbitrage: An Investor's Guide, Keith M. Moore
Risk Management: Approaches for Fixed Income Markets, Bennett W. Golub and Leo M. Tilman
Security Analysis on Wall Street: A Comprehensive Guide to Today's Valuation Methods, Jeffrey C. Hooke
Style Investing: Unique Insight into Equity Management, Richard Bernstein
Using Economic Indicators to Improve Investment Analysis, Second Edition, Evelina Tainer
Valuation: Measuring and Managing the Value of Companies, McKinsey & Company, Inc., Tom Copeland, Tim Koller, and Jack Murrin
Value Investing: A Balanced Approach, Martin J. Whitman

VALUATION WORKBOOK

Step-by-Step Exercises and Tests to Help You Master *Valuation*

McKinsey & Company, Inc.
Tom Copeland
Tim Koller
Jack Murrin
William Foote

JOHN WILEY & SONS, INC.
New York • Chichester • Weinheim • Brisbane • Singapore • Toronto

This publication is designed to provide accurate and authoritative information in regard to the subject matter covered. It is sold with the understanding that the publisher is not engaged in rendering professional services. If professional advice or other expert assistance is required, the services of a competent professional person should be sought.

Library of Congress Cataloging-in-Publication Data:

McKinsey & Company, Inc.
    Valuation : measuring and managing the value of companies / Tom Copeland, Tim Koller, Jack Murrin — 3rd ed.
        p. cm. — (Wiley frontiers in finance)
    Includes index.
    ISBN 0-471-36190-9 (cloth : alk. paper)
    ISBN 0-471-36191-7 (paper ed.)
    ISBN 0-471-39748-2 (cloth with CD)
    ISBN 0-471-39749-0 (CD)
    ISBN 0-471-39750-4 (Web spreadsheet)
    ISBN 0-471-39751-2 (workbook)
        1. Corporations—Valuation—Handbooks, manuals, etc.   I. Copeland, Tom. II. Koller, Tim.   III. Murrin, Jack.   IV. Title.   IV. Series.

    HG4028.V3 C67 2000
    658.15—dc21

                                                                    00-036651

Printed in the United States of America.
10 9 8 7 6 5 4 3 2 1

About the Authors

McKinsey & Company, Inc., is an international top management consulting firm. Founded in 1926, McKinsey & Company, Inc., advises leading companies around the world on issues of strategy, organization, and operations, and in specialized areas such as finance, information technology, and the Internet, research and development, sales, marketing, manufacturing, and distribution.

Tom Copeland was previously a partner and co-leader of corporate finance at McKinsey & Company, Inc., and a professor at UCLA's Anderson School of Management.

Tim Koller is a partner at McKinsey & Company, Inc., and co-leader of its corporate finance and strategy practice. He specializes in restructuring, mergers and acquisitions, and corporate strategy.

Jack Murrin was previously a partner and co-leader of the corporate finance practice at McKinsey & Company, Inc. He has subsequently held senior executive positions at leading financial institutions.

William Foote holds a PhD in Financial Economics from Fordham University and has held teaching positions at Syracuse University and Le Moyne College. He is currently a risk management consultant.

Introduction

The purpose of any workbook is to actively engage of the reader/learner in the transfer of knowledge from author to reader. Although there are many levels at which knowledge can be transferred, *Valuation Workbook* endeavors to provide the following services:

1. A walk-through accompaniment to *Valuation: Measuring and Managing the Value of Companies, Third Edition.*
2. Rearrangement of ideas raised or concluded in the text to spur discussion.
3. Tests of comprehension and skills.

Multiple-choice questions serve to pique your memory as you read the text. Lists and table completions force you to actively rearrange concepts explicitly or implicit within the text. Calculation questions allow you to apply the skills deployed by the authors in accomplishing the analysis called valuation.

If you disagree with wording or answers, then all the better! Our aim has been achieved as you question what you read, we hope, against the background of your own business experience.

Contents

PART ONE

Questions

1

Why Value Value?

This chapter explains why shareholder value is the cornerstone of management and the primary metric for corporate performance. Value comes in different forms and is perceived in various ways by an array of potential stakeholders. Important ideological and legal differences continue to exist among capitalist countries in the wake of the demise of communist economic systems. The rise of hostile takeovers funded by high-yield debt along with anti-inflation monetary and fiscal policy spurred intense focus on earning high returns. More and more employees hold equity in economies that quickly adapt to change.

1. Shareholders and wealth accumulation are most important in the _____, while _____ are more important determinants of value for continental Europe.

    A. Former communist countries, wealth and revenue growth.

    B. United States and United Kingdom, business continuity and inclusive stakeholder governance.

    C. Capital goods sector, representative directors and legal governance structures.

2. Factors critical to the success of the shareholder model of value include:

   A. Convergence of incomes across classes of workers.

   B. Markets for corporate control.

   C. Insolvent social security systems.

   D. Emergence of the global economy.

   E. Increased household assets held as equity.

   F. Equity based management incentives.

   G. Political and social upheaval.

   H. Insolvency of social pension systems.

3. High-yield debt, as a major tool for restructuring companies, occasioned the rise of markets for corporate control during the 1980s.

   A. True, because more money could be found to fund takeovers.

   B. False, because more debt means less control over assets for shareholders.

   C. True, because debt structures required managers to quickly transform free cash flow into high market returns.

   D. False, because LBO transactions eventually fizzled out after the U.S. Congress passed the Financial Institutions Reform, Recovery, and Enforcement Act of 1989.

4. Shareholders can align managers with enterprise goals by:

   A. Requiring more frequent and detailed reporting of operations.

   B. Replacing debt with equity, thus, forcing managers to invest in high-yield operational assets.

   C. Issuing stock options and share grants to managers for achieving various levels of performance.

   D. Reviewing management's hiring choices.

5. Ideological distinctions between labor and capital are blurring. Reasons and implications include:

   A. Real spending by households is falling.

   B. Increasing portions of pension fund assets are moving into equity.

   C. Monopolies are privatizing.

   D. Unionism is declining.

6. Public pensions are failing because:

   A. Governments are mismanaging funds.

   B. There is more claims fraud in public pension schemes.

   C. Contribution rates are declining relative to retiree income claims.

   D. Fund returns fall short of claims experience.

7. The arguments for public pensions to invest in market instruments include:

   A. Inducement of higher contribution premiums.

   B. Attractive returns can be found as funds transit from pay-as-you-go systems.

   C. Government policies are decreasing the retirement age.

   D. Savings need to derive from contribution premiums and investment returns.

8. List three factors that contribute to the U.S. lead in GDP per capita since 1975:

   A. _____

   B. _____

   C. _____

9. Why should shareholder wealth be the most important metric of corporate performance?

    A. Equity holders have the most decision-making authority in the firm.

    B. Most employees have funded pensions.

    C. It shouldn't be. Job growth is the most important social goal on its own.

    D. Managers will limit investment in outdated strategies.

2

The Value Manager

Chapter 1 argues for shareholder value as the primary performance metric. This chapter develops what this means in a practical way as Ralph Demsky walks into a company that obviously needs attention. First, he focuses on the portfolio of opportunities and disasters that comprise EG Corporation. Then, he embarks on a systematic quest to discern where and how value is created and destroyed in EG's many business units. Finally he takes strong positive steps to restructure EG's corporate performance and culture.

1. The most important trait of a value manager is:
   A. To be a coach.
   B. To focus on long-run cash flow returns and incremental value.
   C. To adopt a dispassionate view of corporate activities.
   D. To institutionalize value management throughout the organization.

2. Two aspects of becoming value-oriented are:

   A. _____

   B. _____

3. The situation that best describes EG Corporation as Ralph Demsky becomes CEO is:

   A. A poorly performing, but otherwise well-managed and rationalized set of related businesses.

   B. A mediocre conglomerate comprised of consumer goods, manufacturing, service, property, and finance companies.

   C. A business with some spectacular performers, especially in the finance and manufacturing businesses.

4. List the main virtues and failings of Consumerco, Woodco, Foodco:

Division	Virtues	Failings
Consumerco		
Woodco		
Foodco		

5. What are the analyst's concerns over EG's performance?

   A. _____

   B. _____

   C. _____

6. How did Ralph posture the restructuring project?

   A. Kept it quiet so that no one would be upset over half-baked conclusions and rumors.

    B. Included only financial analysts to speed up the work.

    C. Broadcast the project across the entire company to allay suspicion and include everyone's ideas.

    D. Selected key business leaders along with analysts to take an open-minded but hard-nosed look at sources of value.

7. List the components (hexagon), expected products (performance analyses, scenarios, etc.) and significant results (for each division) of Ralph's approach to analyzing EG's value:

Components	Products	Results

8. Which statement follows from Ralph's restructuring plan?

    A. Maintain investment grade debt rating, capitalize on Consumerco success, and sell Foodco.

    B. Abandon Woodco consolidation, maintain headquarters' control, and expand Foodco.

    C. Sell property and newspaper businesses, push headquarters functions into divisions, and recapitalize by borrowing at lower debt rating.

   D. Develop investor communication strategy, double Consumerco value and maintain headquarters staff to oversee the restructuring plan.

9. Outline Ralph's steps to manage EG's value:

   A. _____

   B. _____

   C. _____

   D. _____

   E. _____

   F. _____

10. How will Ralph put value planning into action?
    A. Require everyone to focus on growth in sales and earnings.
    B. Focus on what drives value for their business—growth, margin, or capital.
    C. Focus on investment in R&D.
    D. Reduce reliance on staff functions.

11. What measures best support Ralph's approach to value planning?
    A. Return on investment (ROI) since this is what shareholders crave.
    B. Payback since this measures how fast a strategy returns cash flow.
    C. Capital growth since this is the measure of the size of the wealth opportunity.
    D. Economic profit since this measures how operations exceed shareholder expectations for return.

12. Discuss why a firmwide hurdle rate cannot meet the goals of an integrated value management program.

    _____

    _____

    _____

    _____

13. Describe the role of the "super CFO."

    A. _____

    B. _____

    C. _____

    D. _____

    E. _____

3

Fundamental Principles of Value Creation

Previous chapters argued that shareholder value and systematic deployment within complex organizations require a revolution in thinking: All planning should revolve around a notion of economic profit. This chapter expands on this notion with an extension of period-to-period economic profit into discounted cash flow and the importance of managing value drivers over time.

1. How does economic profit grow?
   A. Increase invested capital.
   B. Increase shareholder returns expectations.
   C. Decrease shareholder returns expectations.
   D. Increase return on invested capital.

2. How can shutting down a low-profit division actually lower economic profit?
   A. It doesn't, because average return on invested capital (ROIC) will rise.

   B. It can, because the amount of invested capital drops.

   C. It doesn't, because investor return expectations are not changed.

   D. It does, if the low-profit division still outperforms investor return expectations.

3. Why is period-to-period economic profit insufficient to measure performance?

   A. It isn't insufficient since all elements of value creation are represented.

   B. It is insufficient since future performance is not impounded into the metric.

   C. It is insufficient since the cost of capital is not included in the calculation.

   D. It isn't insufficient since the cost of capital is included in the calculation.

4. How are decisions in real and financial markets different?

   A. They really aren't different since each depends on the maximization of future value.

   B. They really aren't different since real market performance is mimicked and replicated in efficient financial markets.

   C. They are different since real market, discounted cash flow maximization must be augmented by financial market preferences for exceeding expectations of intrinsic value.

   D. They are different because real market value optimization does not take into account financial market systematic risk.

5. Why is it important not to over- or underestimate stock market expectations of intrinsic value?

   A. If you overestimate, you may be subject to a takeover.

   B. If you overestimate, you may lack credibility.

   C. If you underestimate, you may be subject to a takeover.

   D. If you underestimate, you may lack credibility.

6. Other than measuring performance and being attuned to market
   perception of value, what else is needed to succeed in growing
   a profitable business?

   A. _____

   B. _____

7. Summarize lessons learned from Fred's Hardware Store:

   A. _____

   B. _____

   C. _____

   D. _____

   E. _____

4

Metrics Mania: Surviving the Barrage of Value Metrics

Up to this point, two measures of value have been proposed: economic profit and discounted cash flow. The real purpose of any value metric must remain to help managers make decisions that maximize value. These decisions can only be implemented if everyone in the company is oriented to and focused on delivering value.

1. List three reasons why economic measures are preferred over accounting measures:

   A. _____

   B. _____

   C. _____

2. Describe the framework for valuation:

   A. _____

   B. _____

C. _____

D. _____

3. List pros and cons of each of the following approaches:

Approach	*Pro*	*Con*
TRS		
MVA		
DCF		
ROIC		
Cost per unit		

4. How can TRS and MVA be combined to assess performance?
   A. Recovering underperformers have low TRS and MVA, while superperformers have high TRS and MVA.
   B. Underachievers have low TRS and MVA, while emerging underperformers have high TRS and low MVA.
   C. Low TRS and low MVA characterize underperformers while emerging underperformers have low TRS and high MVA.
   D. Recovering underperformers have high TRS and low MVA while emerging underperformers have low TRS and high MVA.

5. Problems with price earnings include:
   A. They are future-oriented.
   B. They are consistent with accounting measures.

    C. Can't buy assets with earnings.

    D. Unable to discern differences between long- and short-lived assets.

6. Under what conditions do earnings ratio methods yield the same result as DCF approaches?

    A. They don't ever.

    B. When earnings reflect cash flow but have high invested capital.

    C. When earnings reflect growth and have high invested capital.

    D. When earnings reflect cash flow and have low invested capital.

7. If growth is 10 percent, return on new investment is 20 percent and discount rate is 15 percent, then P/E is:

    A. Not defined.

    B. 1,000.

    C. 100.

    D. 10.

8. P/E rises when:

    A. Growth rises, discount rate falls, reinvestment rate is flat.

    B. Growth falls, discount rate falls, reinvestment rate rises.

    C. Growth exceeds discount rate and reinvestment rate falls short of growth.

    D. Discount rate falls and reinvestment rate rises.

9. List several possible distortions of P/E results.

    A. _____

    B. _____

    C. _____

D. _____

E. _____

10. How can ROIC growth analysis differentiate firms' ability to create or destroy value?

   A. High-ROIC companies can create value by increasing growth rather than earning more ROIC.

   B. Low-ROIC companies can destroy value by increasing growth relative to ROIC.

   C. Growth in invested capital in low-ROIC companies can destroy growth.

   D. Low-growth and low-ROIC companies can destroy value by growing faster than ROIC.

11. Numerical Illustration: Constructing the ROIC growth matrix

   Assume: 15 percent cost of capital, 2-year horizon after which ROIC = Cost of capital and Starting net operating profit less adjusted tax = 1,000. Vary ROIC from 14 percent to 16 percent in 1 percent intervals and growth from 10 percent to 12 percent in 1 percent intervals.

   Step 1: Build DCF model:

Component	*Calculation*	*Explanation*
NOPLAT	1,000	Assumption
Invested capital	$1,000 \times g/\text{ROIC}$	Incremental investment required by growth in operating profit
Cash flow	$1,000 - (1,000 \times g)/\text{ROIC}$	Profit net of investment
DCF value	$1,000 \times (1 - g/\text{ROIC})/(\text{WACC} - g)$	Present value of growing perpetuity

For ROIC = 15 percent and g = 10 percent, the result is:

Component	Calculation
NOPLAT	1,000
Invested capital	667
Cash flow	333
DCF value	6,667

Step 2: Vary NOPLAT growth rate for each of several ROIC rates:

G\ROIC	14%	15%	16%
10%		6,667	
12%			
14%			

Step 3: Interpret results. (For example, explain the results from the point of view of economic profit.)

5

Cash Is King

Does the market really value cash-oriented measures over more traditional accounting reports? This chapter summarizes three decades of research that emphatically answers, Yes. Not only that, but the market takes a long-term view of projected cash flow as well as enabling quick adjustment to announced changes in the ability to generate cash flow and excess returns.

1. How is TRS related to performance?
   A. Highly correlated with absolute earnings growth.
   B. Highly correlated with economic profit.
   C. Highly correlated with deviations from earnings expectations.
   D. Highly correlated with cash flow growth.

2. Note conclusions regarding the relationships among the spread (between return on invested capital and opportunity cost of capital), growth, market-to-book ratio, and DCF:

   A. _____

   B. _____

   C. _____

3. Can accounting treatment mask true earning potential? Summarize the results of research into whether market analysts take a deeper look into the reported earnings.

A. _____

B. _____

C. _____

4. Why does the choice of LIFO or FIFO inventory valuation matter to earnings reports and forecasts?
   A. It doesn't matter when inflation is low or when earnings are reported pretax.
   B. When prices rise, last-in, first-out (LIFO) results in lower earnings.
   C. When prices rise, first-in, first-out (FIFO) results in lower earnings.
   D. When prices fall, FIFO results in lower earnings due to smaller tax payments.

5. How do accounting treatments of mergers and acquisitions affect share value?

A. _____

B. _____

C. _____

6. Which of the following statements summarizes research about whether the market takes a long- or short-term view of the firm?
   A. Oil and gas exploration firms are arbitrarily penalized for a short-term view.
   B. Strategic investment announcements can earn as high as a 1.2 percent return over two days.
   C. The market does not react favorably to the write-off of bad investments.

D. Leverage decreasing transactions results in negative share price impact.

7. Which of the following statements is generally descriptive of efficient markets?

   A. Inefficiency is not consistent with discounted cash flow valuation.

   B. The stock market "always (nearly so) gets it right" (that is, the true value of the asset).

   C. Investors can't beat the market unless they have better information about the value of the asset.

   D. Trading-oriented strategies can beat the market.

   E. Managers should focus on whether the company's stock is 2 percent undervalued this week.

6

Making Value Happen

By now you have been barraged with evidence that the theory of using cash-based valuation methods is well founded, at least implicitly, in market valuation of corporate strategy. You have learned why shareholder value has become the benchmark for identifying and acting on opportunities for growth and profit. You have been guided through two case studies of reinventing and growing businesses (Ralph at EG and Fred's Hardware Store). Now is the time for you to appropriate these anecdotes for use in your own business. This workbook section will provide you with a blueprint for considering the effects of having a value mindset in your organization. Each of the questions can become a slide in a presentation to your managers, employees, or shareholders when outfitted with your own examples of value creation and destruction.

1. Name the key components of making value happen.

   A. _____

   B. _____

C. _____

D. _____

2. Compare and contrast value-based management with more traditional methods.

	Traditional	*VBM*
Strengths		
Weaknesses		

3. What are the dimensions of making value happen (the two-Ms)?

A. _____

B. _____

4. List the key questions for diagnosing and addressing metrics issues.

A. _____

B. _____

C. _____

D. _____

5. What are the implications of a value mindset?

A. _____

B. _____

C. _____

D. _____

E. _____

F. _____

6. Set out an inspirational and value-based mission and vision for your business.

   A. Mission: _____

   B. Vision: _____

7. How do you link, possibly nebulous, value statements to hard quantitative targets?

   A. _____

   B. _____

   C. _____

8. How do you manage a corporate portfolio?

   A. _____

   B. _____

   C. _____

9. Develop corporate themes for your business and compare with the industry leader/role model/incumbent/new entrant, and so on.

Theme	Your business	Comparables
1.		
2.		
3.		
4.		
5.		
6.		
7.		

10. How do you link corporate themes to restructuring alternatives
    for your business?

Theme/Lever	Investor communication	Internal improvements	Disposals	Growth opportunities	Financial engineering
1. Industry shaper					
2. Deal maker		e.g., $5 mm increase in sales staff will increase high-margin deal contribution by $12 mm.			
3. Scarce asset allocator					
4. Skill replicator					
5. Performance manager					
6. Talent agency					
7. Growth asset allocator					

11. Profile your company's growth pattern using the horizon framework below.

Profile/ Horizon	Expand degrees of freedom	Shape your destiny	Create future options
Types of businesses			
Management imperative			
Focus			

12. Detail both hard and soft elements of organizational orientation to value relative to value initiatives for your firm.

Orientation/ Business	Core business	Shape your destiny
Reporting structures		
Decision authority		
Key jobs		
Coordinating change		
Belief in potential value		
Important success criteria		
Leadership style		

13. What are the three uses of value drivers (such as ROIC, growth, cost per unit, asset utilitization, days payables outstanding, revenue/new customer, etc.)?

    A. _____

    B. _____

    C. _____

14. Name three principles for defining value drivers with examples and explanations.

Principle	Driver	Explanation
1.		
2.		
3.		

15. What are the three phases of value driver definition?

    A. _____

    B. _____

    C. _____

16. What are the components of successful business performance management?

    A. _____

    B. _____

    C. _____

17. Discuss several issues with setting targets that link value drivers.

Issue	Resolution

18. What are the key factors in conducting successful performance reviews?

A. What: _____

B. When: _____

C. How: _____

19. What are three motivational levers to encourage individual performance with an example for each?

A. _____

B. _____

C. _____

20. Discuss principles for designing a financial incentive system.

    A. _____

    B. _____

    C. _____

    D. _____

21. Outline the key success factors for implementing value and per-
    formance management programs.

    A. _____

    B. _____

    C. _____

    D. _____

7

Mergers, Acquisitions, and Joint Ventures

Mergers and acquisitions are among the many strategies firms use. Most executives will be involved at least in the analysis of potential candidates or the consideration of various overtures. A merger or acquisition becomes a comprehensive application of how to make value happen.

1. Set out the reasons M&A companies win or lose.

Winners	*Losers*

2. Outline the steps for a successful merger or acquisition.

A. _____

B. _____

C. _____

D. _____

3. What should you consider in establishing a clear vision for the value-adding approach that will work best in the merger or acquisition?

   A. _____

   B. _____

   C. _____

4. How will an M&A affect customer relations?

   A. _____

   B. _____

   C. _____

5. Detail a candidate screening method.

   A. _____

   B. _____

   C. _____

6. Describe synergies (with some examples) useful in analyzing M&A candidates.

Synergy	Characteristics

7. Note some guidelines in conducting a negotiation.

   A. _____

   B. _____

   C. _____

   D. _____

   E. _____

   F. _____

8. Define three steps to successfully manager postmerger issues:

Issue	*Resolution*

9. Compare and contrast mergers with joint ventures according to the following characteristics:

Characteristic	Merger/Acquisition	Joint venture
Overlap		
Ownership split		
Decision making		
Time frame		

10. *Numerical Example:* There are two methods of accounting for mergers: purchase and pooling as governed in the United States by Accounting Principles Board Opinions 16 and 17. *Purchase* accounting writes off goodwill since it requires that the difference between the price paid and the value booked be recorded as goodwill to be amortized over a period of less than 40 years. *Pooling of interest* accounting simply combines corresponding items in the balance sheets of the two organizations.

    How can the choice of these methods affect value? Illustrate your answer by considering the merger of the Electric Car Manufacturer, Inc. with the Electric Car Marketer Corp. into ECMM Enterprises, Inc. Here are the book value balance sheets in ($ million) of the two organizations with fair market value appraisals of property, plant, and equipment. Electric Car Manufacturer, Inc. purchases Electric Car Marketer Corp. for $145 million by issuing debt. WC is working capital (current assets net of non-interest bearing current liabilities) and NFA is net fixed assets.

Electric Car Manufacturer, Inc., Equity		*Electric Car Marketer Corp. Equity*	
WC	10	WC	20
NFA	100	NFA	5
Total	110	Total	25
Fair market value of NFA			30

8

Frameworks for Valuation

Having been (we hope) convinced of the worthiness of shareholder valuation and discounted cash flow in particular, this chapter proposes a set of formulas consistent with valuation principles.

1. List the components of the enterprise-discounted cash flow model.

    A. _____

    B. _____

    C. _____

2. Define free cash flow, net investment, and investment rate:

    A. Free cash flow: _____

    B. Net investment: _____

    C. Investment rate: _____

3. List the components of the economic profit model and reconcile them with the discounted cash flow model.

A. _____

B. _____

C. _____

4. What must a company do to increase its value? Outline three action plans that relate ROIC, WACC, growth, capital, and NOPLAT.

A. _____

B. _____

C. _____

5. Compare and contrast the free cash flow and economic profit models of value. Use three firms as an illustration: one firm earns 10 percent and plows 100 percent of NOPLAT into capital, another earns 12.5 percent and plows 80 percent of NOPLAT into capital, a third earns 12.5 percent and plows 200 percent of NOPLAT into capital; each firm has the same cost of capital. Use the following template for the analysis:

	X	Y	Z
ROIC			
WACC			
Growth			
Investment rate			
NOPLAT			
Net investment	‾‾‾	‾‾‾	‾‾‾
Free cash flow	══	══	══
NOPLAT increase			
ROIC on new capital	‾‾‾	‾‾‾	‾‾‾
EP on new capital			

6. Walk through the Modigliani-Miller formula-based DCF calculation with the following example: $100 in NOPLAT and a
   weighted average cost of capital of WACC = 10 percent; $n =$
   five-year window for competitive position, with an ROIC of 20
   percent and a rate of reinvestment K of 200 percent.

   A. Calculate value of assets in place = NOPLAT/WACC = _____

   B. Calculate value of growth opportunities = Kn(NOPLAT)
      [(ROIC − WACC)/WACC(1 + WACC)] = _____

   C. Calculate total value of firm = In place + Growth values =
      _____

7. Outline the steps in a valuation study.

   A. _____

   B. _____

   C. _____

   D. _____

   E. _____

9

Analyzing Historical Performance

1. What are the starting points and ultimate goals of a comprehensive system for the analysis of historical performance?

   A. Starting points: _____

   B. Ultimate goals: _____

2. What are the determinants of ROIC?

   A. _____

   B. _____

   C. _____

Here is historical data for Freight Way, Inc.:

	1998	1999
Current assets	$ 863	$ 896
Current liabilities	710	818
Debt in current liabilities	1	39
Long term debt	506	408
Total assets	2,293	2,307
Capital expenditures	111	117
Change in deferred taxes	(29)	(20)
Sales	4,056	4,192
Operating expenses	3,307	3,408
General expenses	562	528
Depreciation	139	136
Investment income	5	6
Interest expense	39	30
Miscellaneous income, net	(25)	(4)
Income taxes	(7)	41

The following questions refer to this data.

3. Produce invested capital and NOPLAT statements.

	1998	1999
Invested Capital Statement		
Working capital		
Long term assets	_____	_____
Operating invested capital	══════	══════
Net investment		
Debt		
Equity		
NOPLAT Statement		
Sales		
Operating expenses		
General expenses		
Depreciation	_____	_____
EBIT		
Taxes on EBIT		
Change in deferred taxes	_____	_____
NOPLAT	══════	══════
Provision for income taxes		
Tax shield on interest expense		
Tax on investment income		
Tax on non-operating income	_____	_____
Taxes on EBIT	══════	══════

4. Reconcile the NOPLAT statement to Net Income using the following template:

	1998	1999
Net Income Statement		
Sales		
Operating expenses		
General expenses		
Depreciation	____	____
EBIT		
Investment income		
Investment expense		
Miscellaneous, net	____	____
Earnings before taxes		
Income taxes	____	____
Net income (before extra items)	====	====
Tax rate		
Reconciliation to Net Income Statement		
Net income		
Add: Increase in deferred taxes	____	____
Adjusted net income		
Add: Interest expense after tax	____	____
Income available to investors		
Less: Interest income after tax		
Less: Non-operating income after tax	____	____
NOPLAT	====	====

5. Produce a ROIC tree with the following template:

	1998	*1999*
ROIC Tree		
ROIC		
$\quad$ = (1 – EBIT cash tax rate)		
$\quad\quad$ × Pretax ROIC		
$\quad$ = EBIT/sales		
$\quad\quad$ × Sales/invested capital		
EBIT/sales = 1 – (Operating expenses/sales		
$\quad\quad$ + General expenses/sales		
$\quad\quad$ + Depreciation/sales)		
Sales/invested capital		
$\quad$ = 1/(Operating working capital/sales		
$\quad\quad$ + Long term operating assets/sales)		

6. Develop a free cash flow statement with the following template:

	1999
Free Cash Flow Statement	
NOPLAT	
Depreciation	
Gross cash flow	___
	===
Increase in operating working capital	
Capital expenditures	
Gross investment	___
	===
Free cash flow	
	===
Non-operating cash flow	
Cash flow available to investors	___
	===

7. Develop an Economic Profit Statement. Assume an 11.1 percent weighted average cost of capital.

	1999
Economic Profit	
NOPLAT	
Capital charge	_____
Economic Profit	=====

8. Compare and contrast the free cash flow and economic profit statements.

10

Estimating the Cost of Capital

1. Consistency with the enterprise-discounted cash flow model, requires that the cost of capital must:

   A. _____

   B. _____

   C. _____

   D. _____

2. Identify the steps needed to estimate the cost of capital.

   A. _____

   B. _____

   C. _____

3. What approaches can be used to develop market value weights?

   A. _____

   B. _____

   C. _____

4. Suppose you can issue one of two bonds each carrying a coupon of 10 percent of face value payable at the end of each of two years. The principle repayment for one bond is 100 percent at the end of year two; for the other bond it is 50 percent at the end of year one and 50 percent at the end of year two. The sinking fund earns escrow interest of 10 percent. What is the pretax cost of capital (yield or internal rate of return) on the two bonds if face value is $1,000? Use the following template:

Year	0	1	2
Interest			
Principal			
Net cash flow			
Internal rate of return			

5. What is the effect of taxes on the analysis of the cost of capital of the two bonds described above? Assume a 40 percent tax on ordinary income (revenue and cost components). Use the following template:

Year	0	1	2
Interest received			
Interest paid			
Tax			
Principal			
Net cash flow			
Internal rate of return			

6. Suppose your company has consistently communicated to investors that the firm will take a book value target capital structure approach to financing operations. Currently the capital structure is all equity with a book value of $10,000. Other data is summarized below for various capital structures:

Target debt percent	0%	50%	75%
Target equity percent	100%	50%	25%
Target growth	5%	5%	5%
Target ROIC	20%	20%	20%
Tax rate	40%	40%	40%
Cost of debt	10%	15%	20%
Unlevered beta	0.8	0.8	0.8
Risk-free rate	7%	7%	7%
Market premium	6%	6%	6%

The cost of debt for each capital structure was determined by your firm's investment bankers based on comparable analysis of ratings (spreads over treasury rates) and times-interest-earned ratios for firms similar enough to yours in size, market, and overall business risk.

Use the following template to find the cost of capital. Step 1 calculates the WACC using book value weights. Step 2 recalculates WACC using discounted cash flow weights calculated in step 1. Subsequent iterations recalculate WACC using the previous iteration's estimate of asset value. Iteration ceases when there is no ostensible change to WACC, defined as no change to the second decimal place of the WACC number percentage.

Target debt percent
Target equity percent
Target growth
Target ROIC

Face value of debt
Book value: Equity
Market value: Assets

Tax rate
Cost of debt
Unlevered beta
Levered Beta
Risk-free rate
Market premium
Cost of equity

WACC

NOI
Tax
NOPLAT
Net investment
Free cash flow
Value of assets

NOI is the first period net operating income of a stream of perpetual NOI growing at target growth; net investment is (growth/ROIC) × NOPLAT.

11

Forecasting Performance

You've analyzed the historical record, researched patterns of change in the firm and its markets, estimated the riskiness of the firm as indicated by the return to compensate investors, now to move to the future. The future depends critically on the strategic perspective of the firm as well as the various horizons the firm sets for itself. There is at least a near and far term. More sophisticated analysis will incorporate the multiple horizons of Chapter 3.

1. Outline the basic steps in producing a firm's financial forecast.

   A. _____

   B. _____

   C. _____

   D. _____

   E. _____

2. It has been said repeatedly that adding value translates into an ROIC greater than a WACC. How does this result from competitive

advantages in an evaluation of strategic position? Explore six perspectives:

A. Buyers: _____

B. Sellers: _____

C. Technology: _____

D. Government: _____

E. New entrants: _____

F. Substitute products/services: _____

3. Discuss how customer segmentation, business system, and industry structure analysis contribute to an analysis of value added for the firm.

Here is data for International Machine Tools, Inc. (IMT):

	1995	1996	1997	1998	1999
Current assets	$499	$489	$443	$429	$ 484
Current liabilities	240	236	255	237	369
Debt in current liabilities	25	12	7	21	78
Long-term debt	218	200	244	207	236
Total assets	686	693	598	579	730
Capital expenditures	34	34	16	18	23
Change in deferred taxes	4	(5)	3	2	2
Sales	851	838	754	789	1,029
Operating expenses	626	624	579	592	765
General expenses	151	157	132	134	191
Depreciation	23	24	24	21	26
Investment income	4	2	2	3	2
Interest expense	22	20	19	19	16
Miscellaneous income, net	3	(33)	(75)	—	(70)
Income taxes	18	4	10	11	8

4. Given the historical data, construct three scenarios for IMT value. Develop stories for each growth scenario:

   A. Scenario A: _____

   B. Scenario B: _____

   C. Scenario C: _____

5. Use the following template to list the value-driver assumptions for each scenario:

Driver	A: Low growth	B: Medium growth	C: High growth

6. Use the following template to construct and discuss forecasts for the three scenarios:

Scenario	H 1999	F 2000	F 2001	F 2002
Working capital				
Net fixed assets				
Invested capial				
Net Investment				
Debt				
Equity				
Sales growth				
Net sales				
Operating expense				
General expense				
Depreciation				
Operating income				
Taxes on EBIT				
Change in deferred tax				
NOPLAT				
ROIC				
D/IC				
Eq/IC				
Tax rate				
Interest rate				
Growth (investment/capital)				
Investment rate (Gwh/ROIC)				
EBIT/Sales				
Sales/IC				
WC/sales				
NFA/sales				
Operating expenses/ sales				
SG&A/sales				
Depreciation/sales				
Change in deferred tax/sales				
Free cash flow				

12

Estimating Continuing Value

1. Outline the steps needed to produce an estimate of continuing value.

   A. _____

   B. _____

   C. _____

   D. _____

2. A client explains that her firm's value must be affected by the choice of explicit forecast horizon. Build a model to test her claim. Assume a short horizon of three years, a longer horizon of six years, with explicit forecast growth rate of 11 percent, return on new investment of 18 percent, continuing value growth of 5 percent, and return on new investment of 14 percent, with weighted average cost of capital over both periods of 14 percent. Use the following template. Offer an explanation of the results.

Assumptions	Years 1–3 (%)	Years 4+ (%)
ROIC	18	11
Growth	20	7
WACC	14	12

3-year horizon	1	2	3	CV base
NOPLAT				
Depreciation	___	___	___	
Gross cash flow				
Gross investment	___	___	___	
Free cash flow	===	===	===	
Discount factor				
Present value FCF				
PV FCF 1–3				
PV CV	___			
Total value	===			

5-year horizon	1	2	3	4	5	CV base
NOPLAT						
Depreciation	___	___	___	___	___	
Gross cash flow						
Gross investment	___	___	___	___	___	
Free cash flow	===	===	===	===	===	
Discount factor						
Present value FCF						
PV FCF 1–3						
PV CV	___					
Total value	===					

3. Your client remains skeptical. Why use two different representations of value—free cash flow and economic profit? Show her
   that the present value of economic profit plus beginning invested capital equals the present value of free cash flows.

4. Demonstrate for your client the equivalence between free cash
    flow and economic profit representations of value with a model
    similar to the three-year horizon model. Discuss the similarities,
    differences, and usefulness of each representation. Use the fol-
    lowing template and assumptions:

Assumptions	Years 1–3 (%)	Years 4+ (%)
ROIC	18.00	15.75
Growth	20.00	5.00
WACC	14.00	12.00

3-year horizon	1	2	3	CV base
NOPLAT	10.00			
Net investment	___	___	___	
Free cash flow	═══	═══	═══	
Beginning IC				
Net investment	___	___	___	
New IC	═══	═══	═══	
NOPLAT				
Capital charge	___	___	___	
Economic profit	═══	═══	═══	
Discount factor				
Present value FCF				
Present value EP				
PV FCF 1–3				
PV CV FCF	___			
Total value	═══			
PV EP 1–3				
PV CV				
IC	___			
Total value	═══			

5. Complete the valuation of International Machine Tools, Inc. using data from previous chapters. Include a range of possible outcomes based on growth versus the ROIC positioning of the firm. Assume 33.7 million outstanding shares and an initial beta of 1.73. A template follows with example assumptions:

IMT valuation	H 1999	F 2000	F 2001	F 2002	CV 2003
Working capital	193,000				
Net fixed assets	246,000				
Invested capital	439,000				
Net investment					
Debt	314,000				
Equity	125,000				
Sales growth		10.00%	15.00%	20.00%	
Net sales	1,029,000				
Operating expenses					
General expenses					
Depreciation					
Earnings before interest and tax					
Taxes on EBIT					
Change in deferred tax					
Net operating profit less adjusted tax					
ROIC	13.48%				
D/IC	71.53%	70.00%	68.00%	65.00%	65.00%
Eq/IC	28.47%				
Tax rate	−21.62%	40.00%	40.00%	40.00%	40.00%
Interest rate	5.10%	6.00%	7.00%	7.00%	5.00%
Growth (investment/ capital)					4.00%
Investment rate (Gwh/ROIC)					
EBIT/sales					
Sales/IC					
WC/sales	18.7561%	18.7500%	18.7500%	18.7500%	
NFAOA/sales	23.9067%	24.0000%	24.0000%	24.0000%	

IMT valuation	H 1999	F 2000	F 2001	F 2002	CV 2003
Operating expenses/sales	74.3440%	75.0000%	74.0000%	72.0000%	74.0000%
SG&A/sales	18.5617%	18.6000%	18.6000%	18.0000%	18.6000%
Depreciation/sales	2.5267%	2.5267%	2.5267%	2.5267%	2.5267%
Change in deferred tax/sales	0.194%	0.194%	0.194%	0.194%	0.194%
Free cash flow					
Cost of capital					
Economic profit					
Beta	1.73				
Unlevered beta					
PV factors					
	PV Sums				
PV short term forecast					
Continuing value					
PV continuing value					
Value of IMT					
Debt					
Market value of equity					
Number of shares	33.7				
Stock price					
PV EP 1–3					
Continuing value					
PV CV					
IC					
Value of IMT					

13

Calculating and Interpreting the Results

1. Detail the final steps needed to produce a company's value.

   A. _____

   B. _____

2. Produce a preliminary analysis of the value of IMT using the following three scenarios:

   A. A conservative performance scenario with 3 percent continuing base growth.

   B. A medium performance scenario with 4 percent growth.

   C. An aggressive performance scenario with 6 percent growth.

   The purpose of the analysis is to determine the resilience of IMT's equity market position among its competitors in the long run. This is the first of many steps in the process of determining this position. Keep all other value drivers constant.

3. Identify the pitfalls of valuation analysis in the context of the IMT analysis you just performed.

A. _____

B. _____

C. _____

D. _____

14

Multibusiness Valuation

1. The cost of capital _____ (rises/falls) when business risk _____ (rises/falls), tax rates _____ (rise/fall), new investment _____ (increases/decreases), and new debt _____ (increases/decreases). Why?

2. The cost of equity _____ with business risk and _____. _____ bond rates and tax rates _____ the cost of equity. Why?

3. In projected cash flows for your company, you notice that the market beta is 1.009, nearly the same as the systematic risk index for the average asset in the economy. The debt-to-equity ratio is 1:3. If your company decides to expand its operations by issuing more debt, what will happen to the cost of equity? Use the following template to guide your analysis:

Debt equity	0.33	0.67	1.00	1.50	3.00
Unlevered beta					
Tax rate					
Levered beta					
Unlevered return					
Levered return					
Financial risk					

"Financial risk" is the difference between the levered and un-levered return.

4. A diversified mining and chemical firm has an opportunity to establish a basic chemicals operation in Southeast Asia. Already, project financing partners are willing to stake debt at 20 percent of the total estimated project outlay. Here is data for four basic chemicals firms.

	Dow	Dupont	Olin	United
Beta	1.25	1.15	1.3	1.25
Long term debt ($,000)	3,338,000	3,232,000	474,000	1,408,000
Average stock price	57	28	50	83
Shares outstanding (,000)	275,300	718,450	20,500	68,830
Bond rate	9.75%	9.20%	10.45%	9.75%

What return should the company expect to earn on its 80 percent equity stake in the project?

Detail the final steps needed to produce a company's value.

15

Valuing Dot.coms

---

1. List three issues with valuing dot.com companies and ways to resolve the issues:

Issue	Resolution
A.	
B.	
C.	

2. Let's walk through the valuation for Amazon.com:

   A. List key value drivers that can explain variations in future growth:

Value driver	Relation to growth

B. Set out three scenarios to explain to investors why value can be created by the dot.com:

Driver	Low scenario	Medium scenario	High scenario
Total market size			
Market share			
Average revenue per customer			
Contribution margin per customer			
Average cost of acquisition per customer			
Proportion of customers lost each year			
Sales per capital			
Growth			
Probability			
Date when growth begins			

C. Use the following table to calculate discounted cash flow value for the low scenario:

Item	Calculation	Low scenario
Revenue	Total number × Share × Revenue per customer	
Contribution margin	Total number × Share × Contribution per customer	
Acquisition cost	Total number × Share × Acquisition cost × Churn rate	
EBIT	Contribution margin − Acquisition cost	
Tax	Tax rate × EBIT	
Net operating profit less tax	EBIT − Tax	
Invested capital	Revenue/sales turns	
ROIC	NOPLAT/ invested capital	
Growth	Assumption	
Reinvestment rate	Growth/ROIC	
Free cash flow	NOPLAT × (1 − Reinvestment rate)	
Cost of capital	Assumption	
Continuing value	Free cash flow/ (Cost of capital − Growth)	
Discounted cash flow	Continuing value/ $(1 + \text{Cost of capital})^{10}$	
Number of customers	Total number × Share	
Value per customer	Discounted cash flow/Number of customers	

D. Calculate the remaining scenario values and their expected value.

Item	Low scenario	Medium scenario	High scenario
Revenue			
Contribution margin			
Acquisition cost			
EBIT			
Tax			
Net operating profit less tax			
Invested capital			
ROIC			
Growth			
Reinvestment rate			
Free cash flow			
Cost of capital			
Continuing value			
Discounted cash flow			
Number of customers			
Value per customer			
Expected value			

Expected value is the sum of the products of the probability of each scenario times the scenario value.

16

Valuing Cyclical Companies

1. List two reasons why cyclical firms (e.g., airlines, paper, steel, chemicals) are difficult to value:

   A. _____

   B. _____

2. Outline the steps for calculating cyclical firm value:

   A. _____

   B. _____

   C. _____

   D. _____

3. Follow the steps to value Georgia Pacific. Here is data for the past few years.

	1995	1996	1997	1998	1999
Financial data input					
Current assets	$ 2,595	$ 2,615	$ 2,916	$ 2,645	$ 4,559
Current liabilities	1,764	2,490	3,020	2,648	4,191
Debt in current liabilities	0	0	0	0	0
Long term debt	7,052	6,817	6,460	6,928	8,831
Total assets	12,335	12,818	12,950	12,700	16,897
Capital expenditures	1,503	1,564	892	951	2,609
Change in deferred taxes	10	14	100	38	73
Sales	14,313	13,024	13,094	13,342	17,977
Operating expenses	9,794	9,798	10,209	10,231	13,333
General expenses	1,406	1,475	1,296	1,204	1,670
Depreciation	984	996	1,017	997	1,013
Investment income	—	—	128	24	355
Interest expense	432	459	465	443	495
Miscellaneous income, net	—	(5)	(60)	(15)	—
Income taxes	679	135	106	202	705
Beta	1.33	1.33	1.33	1.33	1.33

A. First, produce invested capital, NOPLAT, free cash flow, and economic profit statements as well as return on invested capital (ROIC) value tree to examine the GP's cyclical character. Develop a normal scenario value for GP. Here are templates for the statements and ROIC value tree:

	1995	*1996*	*1997*	*1998*	*1999*
Invested capital statement					
Working capital					
Long term assets					
Operating invested capital					
Net investment					
Debt					
Equity					
NOPLAT statement					
Sales					
Operating expenses					
General expenses					
Depreciation					
EBIT					
Taxes on EBIT					
Change in deferred taxes					
NOPLAT					
Provision for income taxes					
Tax shield on interest expense					
Tax on investment income					
Tax on non-operating income					
Taxes on EBIT					
Net income statement					
Sales					
Operating expenses					
General expenses					
Depreciation					
EBIT					
Investment income					
Investment expense					
Miscellaneous, net					
Earnings before taxes					
Income taxes					
Net income (before extra items)					
Tax rate					

	1995	*1996*	*1997*	*1998*	*1999*
Reconciliation to net income statement					
Net income					
Add: increase in deferred taxes	___	___	___	___	___
Adjusted net income					
Add: Interest expense after tax	___	___	___	___	___
Income available to investors					
Less: Interest income after tax					
Less: Non-operating income after tax	___	___	___	___	___
NOPLAT	═══	═══	═══	═══	═══
ROIC tree					
ROIC	___	___	___	___	___
= (1 − EBIT cash tax rate) × Pretax ROIC	___	___	___	___	___
= EBIT/Sales × Sales/Invested capital	___	___	___	___	___
EBIT/Sales = 1 − (Operating expenses/Sales + General expenses/Sales + Depreciation/Sales)	___	___	___	___	___
Sales/Invested capital = 1 /(Operating working capital/Sales + Long term operating assets/Sales)	___	___	___	___	___
Change in deferred tax/Sales					
Free cash flow statement					
NOPLAT					
Depreciation	___	___	___	___	___
Gross cash flow	═══	═══	═══	═══	═══

	1995	1996	1997	1998	1999
Increase in operating working capital					
Capital expenditures					
Gross investment					
Free cash flow					
Non-operating cash flow					
Cash flow available to investors					
Cost of capital					
Beta					
Debt/invested capital					
Equity/invested capital					
Cost of debt					
Cost of equity					
Weighted average cost of capital					
Economic profit					
NOPLAT					
Capital charge					
Economic profit					

Value the normal scenario using the following templates:

	Average 1995–1999	F 2000	F 2001	F 2002	CV 2003
Working capital					
Net fixed assets					
Invested capital					
Net investment					
Debt					
Equity					
Sales growth					
Net sales					
Operating expense					
General expense					
Depreciation					
EBIT					
Change in deferred tax					
Net operating profit less adjusted tax					
Net investment					
Free cash flow					
Cost of capital					
Economic profit					
Beta					
Unlevered beta					
PV factors					
PV short term forecast					
Continuing value					
PV continuing value					
Market value of asset					
Debt					
Market value of equity					
Number of shares					
Stock price					

	Average 1995–1999	F 2000	F 2001	F 2002	CV 2003
	Sum				
PV economic profit 1–3					
Continuing value					
PV continuing value					
Invested capital					
Market value of asset					
ROIC					
D/IC					
Eq/IC					
Tax rate					
Interest rate					
Growth (Investment/Capital)					
Investment rate (Growth/ROIC)					
EBIT/Sales					
Sales/IC					
WC/Sales					
NFAOA/Sales					
Operating expenses/Sales					
SG&A/Sales					
Deprecation/Sales					
Change in deferred tax/Sales					

B. Formulate a new-trend scenario using the following pulp and paper industry data:

Sales growth (5-year)	6%
Beta	1.01
Operating expense/sales	70%

Value the new-trend scenario using the following templates:

	Average 1995–1999	F 2000	F 2001	F 2002	CV 2003
Working capital	243,400				
Net fixed assets	10,474,000				
Invested capital	10,717,400				
Net investment					
Debt	7,217,600				
Equity	3,499,800				
Sales growth					
Net sales	14,350,000				
Operating expense					
General expense					
Depreciation					
EBIT					
Taxes on EBIT					
Change in deferred tax					
Net operating profit less adjusted tax					
Net investment					
Free cash flow					
Cost of capital					
Economic profit					
Beta	1.37				
Unlevered beta	0.6043				
PV factors	1				
	PV sums				
PV short term forecast					
Continuing value					
PV continuing value					
Market value of asset					
Market value					
Number of shares					
Stock price					

	Average 1995–1999	F 2000	F 2001	F 2002	CV 2003
	Sum				
PV economic profit 1–3					
Continuing value					
PV continuing value					
Invested capital					
Market value of asset					
ROIC	6.36%				
D/IC	67.34%				
Eq/IC	32.66%				
Tax rate	38.71%				
Interest rate	6.83%				
Growth (investment/ capital)					
Investment rate (Gwh/ROIC)					
EBIT/sales					
Sales/IC					
WC/sales	1.6962%				
NFAOA/sales	72.9895%				
Operating expenses/sales	74.3763%				
SG&A/sales	9.8272%				
Deprecation/sales	6.9784%				
Change in deferred tax/sales	0.391%				

C. Use a framework such as the value hexagon to explain the valuation scenarios and their effect on GP's value.

Components	Products	Results
Current valuation	GP performance from shareholder viewpoint	
"As is" value	Discounted cash flow analysis	
Potential value with internal improvements	Key value drivers Comparable firm and business system analysis	
Potential value with external improvement	Four scenario break up analysis: sale to strategic buyer; flotation; MBO; liquidation	
New growth opportunities	Long-term growth alternatives	
Potential value of financial engineering	Debt management alternatives	

D. Assign probabilities, weight each scenario's stock price, and produce a combined valuation.

Scenario	Probability (%)	Value

17

Valuing Foreign Subsidiaries

1. Outline the steps in the valuation of a foreign subsidiary:

    A. _____

    B. _____

    C. _____

    D. _____

2. Apply the valuation steps to the Montreal, PQ, Canadian-based Quebecor, Inc. The firm's major products and services include advertising, books, daily newspapers, de-inked pulp, wood chips, and woodlands' management. The major subsidiaries of Quebecor, Inc., include: Tej Quebecor (India), Quebecor Printing (USA), Imprimeries Fecome-Quebecor SA (France), and Graficas Monte Alban SA de CV (Mexico) as well as three domestic subsidiaries:

    A. _____

    B. _____

C. _____

D. _____

3. Describe two methods of foreign currency translation:

A. _____

B. _____

4. Suppose that the Southern Company, a U.S. electric utility, is about to translate its Argentinean subsidiary's balance sheet and income statements into U.S. dollars. Argentina is well known for its relatively high inflation rate. Explain the method of foreign currency translation that would be appropriate for Southern Company. Here is hypothetical data from the Argentinean subsidiary. Consider both appreciating and depreciating exchange rates.

Cash and receipt net of NIBCLs	50
Inventory	20
Working capital	70
Net fixed assets	930
	1,000
Debt	720
Equity	280
FX gain (loss)	—
	1,000
Revenue	2,000
Operating costs	(1,760)
SG&A	(100)
Depreciation	(28)
FX gain	—
Operating income	112
Taxes	(45)
NOPLAT	67

ROIC	6.73%
Tax rate	40.00%
Operating increase/sales	5.61%
Sales/capital	2.00
WC/sales	3.50%
NFA/sales	46.50%
Operating expense/sales	88.00%
SG&A/sales	5.00%
Deprecation/sales	1.40%
Debt/capital	72.00%
Equity/capital	28.00%

Note: NIBCL = Non interest bearing current liabilities

5. The French subsidiary of Quebecor wants to value the following French franc cash flows:

	1	2	3	4	5	6
Cash flow (francs)	300	320	410	380	420	450
Nff (foreign)	6.9375%	8.4375%	10.3375%	11.6375%	12.8375%	13.9375%
Ncd (domestic)	7.5625%	8.6625%	9.6625%	10.7625%	11.9625%	12.9625%

Provided are the forecasted nominal French franc and Canadian dollar one-year-forward interest rates. The current Canadian dollar-to-French franc spot rate is 2.27 C$/Ff. The U.S. cost of capital is 14 percent over this forecast period. Your supervisor also needs an explanation of the process whereby you arrived at the present value for her presentation to the board of directors.

6. Describe four reasons parity works:

    A. _____

    B. _____

    C. _____

    D. _____

7. The U.S. subsidiary of NorskAuto AB must purchase Norwegian parts to assemble antilock braking systems. Suppose that on April 10, 2000, the factory agrees to buy parts valued at NKR 1,000,000 from Norwegian producers on June 23, 2000. The factory purchaser believes that the dollar will depreciate further before the sale date, making the NKRs it must buy more expensive. The currency prices facing the firm on April 10 are (fictitious, of course) 0.7288 USD/NKR on 125,000 NKR/contract June futures. How can the U.S. importer lock in the dollar costs regardless of whether the dollar depreciates or appreciates relative to the NKR? Fill in the following script to answer the question:

    > To hedge the price of acquiring NKR _____, the factory must enter into _____ NKR/125,000 NKR/contract = _____ futures contracts. Since the factory is taking a long position, its futures prices will be the _____ (bid/ask) price. To see how this simple strategy locks in dollar costs, consider two scenarios: The NKR depreciates by 10 percent versus the dollar, and the NKR appreciates by 10 percent versus the dollar.

    > In the first scenario, the dollar appreciates and the NKR _____ to _____ USD/NKR. In this case the hedged dollar costs are

    > Unhedged − Futures profit (loss)
    > = (NKR _____) (_____ USD/NKR)
    >   − _____ contracts (125,000 NKR/contract)
    >   (_____ USD/NKR − _____USD/NKR)
    > = USD_____.

In the second case, the NKR _____ while the dollar depreciates. The expected spot price will be 10 percent higher than the futures forecast on April 10, _____ USD/NKR. The hedged dollar costs are:

Unhedged – Futures profit (loss)

= (NKR _____) (_____ USD/NKR)

   – _____ contracts (125,000 NKR/contract)

   (_____ USD/NKR – _____ USD/NKR)

= USD _____ .

Whether the dollar depreciates or not, the dollar cost is locked in. The straight hedged cost is NKR _____ (_____ USD/NKR) = USD _____ .

8. A U.S. gas marketing company is bidding on the delivery of British originated (North Sea) natural gas to a Norwegian chemical company in 90 days for USD 1,000,000. The following rates (again, fictitious) are quoted by the Norwegian chemical company's London bank:

	NKR	*USD*	*GBP*
90-day Eurocurrency rates in following currencies	0.0575	0.06125	0.050625
Spot rates currency/USD	1.942		0.609

Should the Norwegian chemical firm contract directly with the British in GBP producer or work with the U.S. gas marketer in USD?

18

Valuation Outside of the United States

1. What are the ways in which accounting practices affect the calculation of an enterprise's value?

   A. Format: _____

   B. Consolidation: _____

   C. Business combinations: _____

   D. Goodwill: _____

   E. Inventory valuation methods: _____

   F. Fixed asset valuation and depreciation methods: _____

   G. Discretionary reserves: _____

   H. Income tax: _____

   I. Foreign currency translation: _____

   J. Pension accounting: _____

2. List several hurdles to restatement of accounting statements:

   A. _____

   B. _____

   C. _____

   D. _____

3. In the example of the hypothetical German company, show the correspondence of the statements to each of the accounting differences you outlined in question one by completing the following report:

   A. Format for the presentation of accounting objects. Notice that long-term assets and liabilities are presented _____, followed by _____ items. Cash sales is recorded against changes in _____ inventory. Either production or _____ presentations could have been made. Notes to the financial statements and a management report are _____ required.

   B. Consolidation of subsidiaries and minority interests. Consolidation is required for parent companies that exercise control over subsidiary companies with over _____ percent of voting rights. Both _____ and significant control, as measured by _____, consolidations are supported.

   C. Business combinations. _____ and _____ purchase methods are used.

   D. Goodwill. The goodwill amortized (*Gesamt-Abschreibungen*) is a _____ expense over a _____ year period. Goodwill is not reported under this exhibit's total assets (*Gesamtvermogen*).

   E. Inventory valuation methods. *Vorrate* is recorded at lower of _____ or _____. Inventory must be written down if market values _____ historical cost. Inventory reserves can be used to anticipate future price changes.

F. Fixed asset valuation and depreciation methods. Straightline and declining-balance methods are the most common depreciation methods. Conservative tax tables are used to extrapolate _____ for financial accounting. Thus, there is practically no difference between financial and tax _____, so that deferred taxes do not normally exist. Tangibles are recorded at _____ or _____ cost. Capital expenditures are the _____ in property, plant, and equipment plus _____.

G. Income tax. The commercial balance sheet determines the tax liability. Higher tax rates are applied to _____ profits; a lower rate is used for _____ profits. The 50 percent tax rate is reduced by deductible municipal rates. Taxes on EBIT derive from _____, shields on _____ expense, tax on interest income, and _____ income.

H. Foreign currency translation. A variety of translation methods are available: _____, _____, _____, monetary/non-monetary. Gains and losses may be transmitted either through _____ or _____ statements.

I. Pension accounting. _____ for uncertain obligations are typically understated since they ignore accruals for _____ and they exclude future payroll increases in the actuarial _____ obligations.

4. Perform the following operations with data from June 2, 2000:

A. Borrow USD 1 today and earn USD 1 + _____ in one year.

Borrow GBP/USD _____ today and earn (GBP/USD _____)(1 + _____) in one year.

B. In one year GBP/USD is expected to be _____.

C. Thus, USD equivalent earned in one year is GBP _____ / GBP/USD _____ or _____.

D. Your conclusion about risk-free rates across heavily arbitraged currency borders is _____.

19

Valuation in Emerging Markets

The valuation of nominal versus real cash flows headlines the many issues addressed in this chapter. Nominal cash flows for emerging market companies are affected by often abrupt changes in open economy, monetary and fiscal policy, spot and forward movements in capital and foreign currency markets, as well as a host of problems associated with liquidity, sovereign debt, repatriation of dividends and local taxation, import-export quota, and exchange rate translation. The problems following will focus on real and nominal cash flow forecasts and their valuation.

1. List effects of volatile inflation on estimating cash flows:

    A. _____

    B. _____

    C. _____

2. Discuss the need for both real and nominal forecasts:

    A. Real: _____

    B. Nominal: _____

3. Outline the steps in calculating cash flows:

A. _____

B. _____

C. _____

D. _____

E. _____

F. _____

G. _____

H. _____

I. _____

4. The effect of differential growth on revenues can be examined by splitting revenue growth into real and inflation components. Forecast revenue so that Revenue (year 2) = Revenue (year 1) × (1 + real growth rate) × (1 + inflation rate). Here are the assumptions for the analysis:

Assumptions	1	2	3	4	Continuing value
Real revenue growth		10%	10%	10%	5%
EBITDA/revenue	30	30	30	30	30
Tax rate	50	50	50	50	50
Inflation rate	20	50	70	100	20
Depreciation/beginning net PPE	20	20	20	20	20
Capital expenditure/revenue	8	8	8	8	8
Working capital/revenue	20	20	20	20	20
Inflation index	1.00	1.50	2.55	5.10	6.12

A. Calculate nominal net income, invested capital, and free cash flow:

Income, assets, cash flow	Nominal				Continuing value
	1	2	3	4	
Revenue					
EBITDA					
Depreciation	___	___	___	___	___
Operating income					
Tax	___	___	___	___	___
Net income	═══	═══	═══	═══	═══
Working capital					
Beginning net PPE					
Less: Depreciation					
Plus: Capital expenditure					
Ending net PPE	___	___	___	___	___
Invested capital (working capital + beg PPE)	═══	═══	═══	═══	═══
Net income					
Plus: Depreciation					
Less: Working capital change					
Less: Capital expenditure	___	___	___	___	
Free cash flow	═══	═══	═══	═══	

B. Calculate net income, invested capital, and free cash flow
   by deflating revenues only:

Income, assets, cash flow	Unadjusted real forecast				Continuing value
	1	2	3	4	
Revenue					
EBITDA					
Depreciation	———	———	———	———	———
Operating income					
Tax	———	———	———	———	———
Net income	═══	═══	═══	═══	═══
Working capital					
Beginning net PPE					
Less: Depreciation					
Plus: Capital expenditure					
Ending net PPE	———	———	———	———	———
Invested capital (working capital + beg PPE)	═══	═══	═══	═══	═══
Net income					
Plus: Depreciation					
Less: Working capital change					
Less: Capital expenditure	———	———	———	———	
Free cash flow	═══	═══	═══	═══	

C. Calculate nominal translation to real (nominal revenue/inflation index, etc.) net income, invested capital, and free cash flow:

Income, assets, cash flow	Nominal to real translation				Continuing value
	1	2	3	4	
Revenue					
EBITDA					
Depreciation	____	____	____	____	____
Operating income					
Tax	____	____	____	____	____
Net income	====	====	====	====	====
Working capital					
Beginning net PPE					
Less: Depreciation					
Plus: Capital expenditure					
Ending net PPE	____	____	____	____	____
Invested capital (working capital + beg PPE)	====	====	====	====	====
Net income					
Plus: Depreciation					
Less: Working capital change					
Less: Capital expenditure	____	____	____	____	
Free cash flow	====	====	====	====	

D. Compare the approaches using the following results template:

Results	1	2	3	4	Continuing value
Real net income					
Real cash flow					
Beginning PPE/revenue					
Net income/invested capital					

5. Given the free cash flow developed previously, compare discounted cash flow. Use 8 percent real cost of capital:

   A. The continuing value nominal weighted cost of capital is
   _____ .

   B. The continuing value nominal growth rate is _____ .

   C. Calculate nominal DCF:

	1	2	3	4	Continuing value
Free cash flow					
Continuing value					
Discount factor					
PV of cash flow					
DCF					
Real WACC	□				
Nominal WACC					
Continuing value growth					

Free cash flow for years 1 to 4 is taken directly from the free cash flow forecast in the previous question. Continuing-value

free cash flow is discounted by the nominal WACC net of
the nominal growth rate in perpetuity to arrive at the
continuing-value number.

D. Calculate unadjusted real forecast DCF:

	1	2	3	4	Continuing value
Free cash flow					
Continuing value					
Discount factor					
PV of cash flow					
DCF					
Real WACC					
Nominal WACC					
Continuing value growth					

E. Calculate nominal to real translation DCF:

	1	2	3	4	Continuing value
Free cash flow					
Continuing value					
Discount factor					
PV of cash flow					
DCF					
Real WACC					
Nominal WACC					
Continuing value growth					

F. Comment on the results: _____ .

20

Using Option Pricing Methods to Value Flexibility

---

1. Graph the following risk positions for strike price X with an example of each:

   A. Long forward position

   B. Short forward position

   C. Long call

   D. Short call

   E. Long put

   F. Short put

2. Graph the following strategies:

   A. Money spread: Purchase a call (or put) above and sell a call (put) below the current underlying asset price.

   B. Strip: Purchase two puts and one call of the same maturity on the same asset.

   C. Spark spread option: Buy an option to call gas (swing gas) at $20/MWh (equivalent) and sell an option to call power (interruptible power) at $30/MWh.

3. Suppose a stock is quoted at $50, and a 90-day put with $40 strike price written on the stock is worth $3.05; 90-day T-bills yield 7.1 percent. Assume that the stock does not pay dividends, and Federal Reserve policy appears to be relatively stable over the 90-day period. Show that you can create and price the corresponding call option using the following strategy:

   A. Purchase (go long) a share of stock _____

   B. Purchase 1 put call _____

   C. Borrow the present value of the strike price _____

4. Compare and contrast financial and real options using the following framework:

Input	Oil reserve	Stock option
Underlying asset value		
Exercise price		
Time to expiration of option		
Riskless rate		
Variance in underlying asset value		
Dividend yield		

5. Suppose a mining firm in the United States wants to value an open-pit copper mine in Southeast Asia. Geologists expect the mine to tap out its reserve in 3 years at the rate of 150 million tons next year, 100 million the next year, and the remainder of

the 300 million ton reserve in the third year. The copper ore mine mouth net operating profit less adjusted taxes is currently $0.10 per ton mined. Copper price percentage changes vary with a standard deviation of 20 percent per year; this represents the only uncertainty of any importance to the mine. The real rate of interest on 3 year treasury instruments is 3 percent.

A. Forecast the copper margin at the mine over the 3 years using the following templates and a binomial tree representation of copper margin uncertainty:

Riskless rate	Real rate
Cu margin	Average copper margin
Sigma	Standard deviation of spot copper prices
Up	Exp(Sigma × Years)
Down	1/up
Salvage/ton	Assumption

Years is the time frame of the standard deviation of copper prices (assume 1 year for per-annum volatility).

The resulting binomial tree is (with the first computational branch illustrated):

Cu Margin			
0	**1**	**2**	**3**
0.10	0.10 up		
	0.10 down		

B. Forecast NOPLAT. This is the forecasted copper margin times the amount of copper mined. Begin with the reserve schedule:

Year	1	2	3
Reserves (beginning of period)	[Starting amount]	[Starting amount – Year 1 mined]	[Year 2 reserve – Year 2 mined]
Mined (end of period)	150	100	50

Next compute the NOPLAT tree by multiplying the amount mined each year times the binomial tree copper margin forecast.

		NOPLAT		
0	**1**	**2**	**3**	
	18.321			
	12.281			

C. Third, compute the straight value of the mine, that is, the value of mine without salvage. Use the following template. Start at the end of the mine's life, at period 3. The value of the mine is simply the NOPLAT to be received at the end of period 3. Then fold the valuation back from period 3 to period 2 using the following formula applied to value in period 2 after 2 up jumps in copper margin:

$$V(2,\text{upup}) = \frac{\begin{bmatrix} (\text{Probability\_up} \times V(3,\text{upupup}) + \\ \text{Probability\_down} \times V(3,\text{upupdown}) \end{bmatrix}}{(1+r) + \text{NOPLAT}(2,\text{upup})}$$

Probability_up = (1 + r-down)/(up-down) and
Probability_down = 1 – Probability_down.

Thus,

$$V(2, \text{upup}) = \frac{(0.53 \times 9.11 + 0.47 \times 6.12)}{1.03 + 14.92} = 22.38.$$

Similarly compute the other nodes.

Mine value without salvage years		
1	2	3
	22.38	9.111
		6.107

D. Fourth, find the value of salvage option again starting at the end of the option's life and working back to year 0.

At the end of period 3, the value of the put option equals the Max(margin × remaining reserves − NOPLAT, 0). The value at nodes prior to period 3 is found in ways similar to the value of the straight mine (without salvage value). For example, after 1 down and 1 up jump in the copper margin, the value of the put option is 0.19. This is found by finding the maximum of the intrinsic value of the option to abandon the mine versus the value to keep the mine open through period 3 (keep the salvage option alive). The formula is:

$$S(2, \text{downup}) = \text{Max} \begin{cases} \text{Margin}(2, \text{downup}) \times \text{Reserve}(2) - V(2, \text{downup}), \\ \dfrac{[\text{Probability\_up} \times S(3, \text{downupup}) + \text{Probability\_down} \times S(3, \text{downdowndown})]}{1 + (r)} \end{cases}$$

Where, S is the value of salvage and V is the value without salvage. The first term is the intrinsic value of salvage, while the second term is the value of keeping the salvage option alive. Using the data from the previous binomial trees, we have:

$$S(2, \text{downupup}) = \text{Max}\left[\begin{array}{c} 0.10 \times 150 - 15, \\ \dfrac{(0.53 \times 0 + 0.47 \times 0.41)}{1.03} \end{array}\right] = 0.19$$

Salvage value years		
1	*2*	*3*
	0.19	
		0.41

E. The value of the mine with an abandonment option is:

Value without salvage	
Salvage value	_____
Total	======

21

Valuing Banks

---

1. The following is a simplified balance sheet for a bank with associated yields:

Community Bank			
			Rate
Assets			
	Cash reserves	$ 150	7%
	Loans	850	11%
	Total assets	$1,000	
Liabilities			
	Deposits	$ 950	4%
	Equity	50	
	Total liabilities	$1,000	

The bank does not earn income on the Federal Reserve cash balance. Cash non-interest expenses are $40. The tax rate is 40 percent.

A. Calculate net income with the income model:

```
        Interest income
        Interest expense
        Other expenses              _____

        Net profit before tax
        Taxes                       _____

        Net income                  ======
```

B. Calculate net income with the spread model:

```
        Loan spread
        Deposit spread
        Equity credit
        Reserve debit
        Expenses                    _____

        Net profit before tax
        Taxes                       _____


        Net income                  ======
```

C. Compare the two methods:

_____

_____

_____

_____

2. Develop a bank valuation forecast narrative:
    The model starts with a forecast of _____ growth. Loans are
    then determined by a _____ ratio. _____ reserves work
    from a cash reserve-to-total deposit ratio, reflecting Federal Re-
    serve policy. Premises, equipment, and other assets are required
    to support deposits directly and loans indirectly. Investments
    are related to cash reserves. Given a level of _____, a man-
    agerially determined _____ to total asset relationship is
    determined. Federal Funds Purchased balances _____.
    _____ balances the balance sheet. Non-interest income and
    expense are related to deposit size. Forecasts of interest rates
    drive the _____, term borrowing, investment, and
    _____ rates.

3. Use the equity method to value Neighborhood Bank System, Inc. Here is a very simplified version of Neighborhood Bank System's balance sheet, income statement, and average rates for 1999:

	1999 Amount	*Rate (percent)*
Income statement		
Interest income	$ 66,919	8.11
Interest expense	(25,221)	3.52
Net interest income	41,698	4.59
Other income	5,120	
Other expenses	(26,498)	
Net profit before tax	20,320	
Taxes	(7,721)	38.00
Net income	$ 12,598	
Balance sheet		
Cash reserves	$ 32,411	
Investment securities	378,520	6.93
Net loans	446,135	9.12
Net premises, other assets	25,526	
Less: Provision for credit losses	(6,281)	
Total assets	$876,311	
Interest bearing deposits	$552,892	3.29
Non-interest bearing deposits	98,587	
Other short term liabilities	6,102	
Federal funds purchased	57,300	4.00
Term borrowings	105,550	4.49
Liabilities	820,431	
Shareholders' equity	55,880	13.48
Total	$876,311	

Depreciation is $1.434 million for 1999. Beta for the firm's equity is 1.20.

A. First, develop a set of assumptions about beta and key ratios using the following template:

	Historical 1999	Explicit forecast period 2000	2001	2002	CV period 2003
Neighborhood Banking System, Inc. **Key ratios and assumptions**					
Loan/deposit					
Other liabilities/ total assets					
Term borrowing/ total assets					
Liabilities/total assets					
Cash reserves/investment					
Cash reserves/deposits					
Deposit growth					
Provision for loan loss/ net loans					
Premises, other assets/ deposits					
Other income/deposits					
Other expenses/deposits					
Depreciation/net premises					
Beta					

B. Next, calculate net income using the template on page 105.
C. Now calculate the balance sheet using the template on page 106.

Income statement

| | 1999 | | Explicit forecast period | | | | | | CV Period | |
| | | | 2000 | | 2001 | | 2002 | | 2003 | |
	Amount	Rate	Amount	Rate	Amount	Rate	Amount	Rate	Amount	Rate
Interest income	——		——		——		——		——	
Interest expense										
Net interest income	——		——		——		——		——	
Other income	——		——		——		——		——	
Other expenses										
Net profit before tax	——		——		——		——		——	
Taxes	——		——		——		——		——	
Net income	≡≡		≡≡		≡≡		≡≡		≡≡	

Balance sheet

| | Explicit forecast period | | | | | | CV period | | | |
| | 1999 | | 2000 | | 2001 | | 2002 | | 2003 | |
	Amount	Rate	Amount	Rate	Amount	Rate	Amount	Rate	Amount	Rate
Cash reserves										
Investment securities										
Net loans										
Net premises, other assets										
Less: Provision for credit losses										
Total assets										
Interest bearing deposits										
Non-interest bearing deposits										
Other short term liabilities										
Federal funds purchased										
Term borrowings										
Liabilities										
Shareholders' equity										
Total										

D. Finally calculate equity cash flows and the value to equity holders:

Equity cash flow and value		*Explicit forecast period*			*CV period*
	1999	*2000*	*2001*	*2002*	*2003*
Net income					
Depreciation					
Less: Increase in assets					
Plus: Increase in liabilities	_____	_____	_____	_____	_____
Equity cash flow	══════	══════	══════	══════	══════
Present value factor					
PV equity cash flows					
PV continuing value					
Market value of equity					
Number of shares					
Stock price					

22

Valuing Insurance Companies

1. Outline the steps needed to value an insurance company:

   A. _____

   B. _____

   C. _____

   D. _____

2. Summarize Transamerica's historical experience:
   A. Revenue developments _____
   B. Expense developments _____
   C. Free cash flow experience _____
   D. Benefits versus premium _____

3. Characterize an alternative scenario for Transamerica using the following drivers for years 1999–2001 and separately in perpetuity:
   A. Net premium growth _____
   B. Investment income rate _____

Use the following forecast ratios and other drivers to project future cash flows and economic profit:

$ million and %	1999	2000	2001	2002	CV
Operations					
Net premium growth	3.0%	3.5%	3.0%	2.5%	2.0%
Investment income/ investments	7.5	7.5	7.5	7.0	7.0
Capital gain/total invested	0.1	0.1	0.1	0.1	0.1
Capital gain (inc. unreal'd gain)/total invested	0.1	0.1	0.1	0.1	0.1
Interest (lending) income growth	6.0	6.0	6.0	6.0	6.0
Other income growth	2.0	2.0	2.0	2.0	2.0
Expenses					
Net claims/net premiums	155.0	153.0	153.0	153.0	153.0
Amort of def acq cost/net premium	14.6	14.6	14.6	14.6	14.6
Other expense/other revenue	144.0	140.0	140.0	140.0	140.0
Taxes and financing					
Corporate tax rate	35.0	35.0	35.0	35.0	35.0
Taxes/pre-tax income	35.0	35.0	35.0	35.0	35.0
Interest expense/debt	6.5	6.5	6.5	6.5	6.5
Common dividends/net income	35.0	35.0	35.0	35.0	35.0
Working capital					
Operating cash/total revenues	2.0	2.0	2.0	2.0	2.0
Accounts receivable/net premiums	117.2	117.2	117.2	117.2	117.2
Net fixed assets/total revenues	54.9	54.9	54.9	54.9	54.9
Def policy acq cost/net premiums	112.7	112.7	112.7	112.7	112.7
Growth of separate assets	8.0	8.0	8.0	8.0	8.0
Interest (lending) income/other assets	9.5	9.5	9.5	9.5	9.5
Accounts payable/total revenues	37.2	37.2	37.2	37.2	37.2
Other liabilities/total revenues	0.0	0.0	0.0	0.0	0.0
Reserves and investments					
Net cash benefit paid/ premiums	140.0	140.0	140.0	140.0	140.0
Net additions to reserves/premiums	11.0	11.0	11.0	11.0	11.0
Investments/provisions and reserves	101.0	101.0	101.0	101.0	101.0

4. Forecast the income statement, balance sheet and cash flow/
    economic profit statements using the following templates (with
    1999 included for validation):

Income statement ($ million)	1999	2000	2001	2002	CV
Net premium income	1,902				
Interest income (investments)	2,405				
Realized capital gains	32				
Interest income (loans)	747				
Other revenues	1,266				
Total revenues	6,353				
Benefits and claims	(2,949)				
Amortization of acquisition costs	(278)				
Other expense	(1,823)				
Total operating expenses	(5,049)				
Interest expense	(533)				
Income before exceptional provisions	771				
Exceptional provisions	—				
Income before taxes	771				
Income taxes	(270)				
Income before extraordinary items	501				
Extraordinary items	—				
Net income	501				
Beginning retained earnings	3,746				
Net income	501				
Common dividends	(175)				
Preferred dividends	—				
Potential dividends	(319)				
Adjustments	—				
Ending retained earnings	3,753				

Balance sheet ($ million)	1999	2000	2001	2002	CV
Assets					
Insurance investments	32,067				
Cash and short term investments	127				
Excess marketable securities	—				
Accounts receivable	2,230				
Net tangible fixed assets	3,488				
Intangible assets	423				
Deferred policy acquisition costs	2,144				
Separate account assets	9,829				
Other assets	7,866				
Total assets	58,174				
Liabilities and shareholders' equity					
Total debt	8,200				
Accounts payable	2,363				
Separate account liabilities	9,829				
New debt	(1,034)				
Total liabilities	19,358				
Provisions and reserves	32,388				
Minority interest	715				
Preferred shares	—				
Common shares	70				
Share premium	—				
Net unrealized capital gains	1,943				
Retained earnings	3,746				
Transfers and other movements	(46)				
Total shareholders' equity	5,713				
Total liabilities and shareholders' equity	58,174				
Beginning provisions and reserves	32,388				
Increase in reserves	209				
Increase in provisions	17				
Ending provisions and reserves	32,614				

Cash flow statement ($ million)	1999	2000	2001	2002	CV
Net premium income	1,902				
Amortization of deferred acquisition costs	(278)	___	___	___	___
Insurance profit before benefits and claims	1,625				
	—				
Benefits and claims	(2,949)				
Increase in insurance liabilities and reserves	—	___	___	___	___
Net cash benefits and claims paid	(2,949)	___	___	___	___
Net insurance cash flow	(1,324)				
Net interest income	2,405				
Other income	2,013				
Other expense	(1,823)				
Exceptional income and provisions	—				
Income taxes	(270)				
Realized capital gains	32				
Extraordinary items	—	___	___	___	___
Cash from operations	1,034				
Other cash sources					
Increase in accounts payable and other liabilities	(31)	___	___	___	___
Total other cash sources	(31)				
Cash uses					
Increase in investments	(1,589)				
Increase in cash and short-term investments	(32)				
Increase in accounts receivable	(24)				
Increase in fixed assets	(39)				
Increase in intangible and other assets	579				
Increase in deferred acquisition costs	49	___	___	___	___
Total cash uses	(1,056)	___	___	___	___
Cash flow before financing	2,059	___	___	___	___

Cash flow statement $ million)	1999	2000	2001	2002	CV
Increase in debt	(1,032)				
Minority interest	—				
Increase in preferred stock	—				
Interest expense	(533)				
Equity cash flow	494				
Dividends	175				
Potential dividends	319				
Increase in common stock and adjustments to retained earnings	—				
Equity cash flow	494				

Economic profit statement ($ million)	1999	2000	2001	2002	CV
Economic profit					
Beginning equity	5,706				
Return on beginning equity	8.8%				
Cost of equity	9.4%				
Spread	−0.6%				
Economic profit	(36)				
Economic profit (adj for unrealized cap gains)					
Beginning equity (less unrealized capital gains)	3,763				
Return on beginning equity	13.3%				
Cost of equity	9.4%				
Spread	3.9%				
Economic profit	147				

5. Estimate continuing value:

_____

_____

_____

_____

6. Estimate equity value using the following template:

$ million	1999	2000	2001	2002	CV
Cash flow	494				
Economic profit adjusted for unrealized gains	147				
PV factor	0.9141				
PV of CF	451				
PV of EP	134				

$ million	DCF	EP
Operating value		
Beginning equity (less unrealized gains)	____	____
Equity value		
Plus: unrealized gains	____	____
Estimated equity value		
Market value of equity		
Percent difference between market and estimate		

Again, 1999 is included for validation. Be sure to deduct unrealized gains from beginning equity (1998) since cash flows do not recognize these amounts. You know you are very probably right when the EP equity value = DCF equity value. If they diverge go first to the cash flow statement and be sure that all balance sheet changes reflect (not ratio forecast) changes directly from the forecasted balance sheet. Then, be sure that income statement substitutions were made correctly.

PART TWO

Answers

1

Why Value Value?

---

1. B

2. B, C, E, F, H

3. C

4. B, C

5. B, C

6. C, D

7. B, D

8. A. factor productivity
   B. high corporate financial returns
   C. ability to progress continually

9. A, B, D

2

The Value Manager

1. D

2. A. Restructuring to unleash trapped value
   B. establish value creation priorities and investor/employee communications

3. B

4.

Division	Virtues	Failings
Consumerco	Dominant market share and strong brand	But not enough to boost overall EG performance
Woodco	Plan for common sales and marketing	High operating costs and uneven performance
Foodco	Good brand and aggressive capital base	Small player

5. A. EG lags its peers and the market
    B. brand is not turning over returns
    C. probably a good break-up play.

6. D

7.

Components	Products	Results
Current valuation	EG performance from shareholder viewpoint	Woodco acquisitions accompanied by stock price downturns. Consumerco growing at rate of inflation only. Consumerco cash flow subsidized Woodco and Foodco projects. Foodco's high capital requirements fizzled earnings growth. Analysts consistently revised EG forecasts downwards.
As is value	Discounted cash flow analysis	Historical value is below EG market value. Foodco value is less than the invested capital: Focus is on growth over return. Consumerco cash flow comprises most of EG's value: Focus is on cash flow. Woodco consolidation adds significant component of value. Headquarters' costs are a large drag on value.

(continued)

Components	Products	Results
Potential value with internal improvements	Key value drivers Comparable firm and business system analysis	Consumerco holding prices down; not investing in R&D; sensitive to sales; salesforce lacks productivity; relatively high cost of goods sold.
		Woodco needs to focus on higher margins and less on growth; do not stray out of mass production basic furniture market.
		Foodco has no advantages in its extremely competitive markets; cut back to only profitable locations; franchise to decrease cost of capital.
		Eliminate 50% of overhead costs.
Potential value with external improvement	Four scenario break-up analysis: sale to strategic buyer; flotation; MBO; liquidation	Simple breakup based on comparable Pes, Market-to-book, and so forth, would not outperform current market value.
		Consumerco is natural buy-out and acquisition target with high cash flow.
		Foodco's real estate holdings make it a partial liquidation candidate.
		Sell consumer finance portfolio since operating costs exceeds net interest income.
		Because of consolidation, Woodco would not attract a buyer for the risk of reconstructing Woodco's many components.
		EG is a takeover target with Consumerco's cash flow.
New growth opportunities	Long-term growth alternatives	Put acquisition and other growth initiatives on the agenda.
		Incubate Consumerco's new businesses.
		Promote long-term growth imperative associated with each of the identified restructuring initiatives.

Components	Products	Results
Potential value of financial engineering	Debt management alternatives	Use stable cash flows to support more debt. Raise debt to repurchase shares or pay special dividends; find ways to return cash to shareholders.

8. C

9. A. focus performance on value
   B. develop value-based performance targets
   C. restructure incentives
   D. evaluate strategic decisions based on value
   E. communicate value to investors
   F. reshape CFO role

10. B

11. D

12. Hurdle rates should reflect the risk undertaken with operations. This implies that if two divisions have different risks, then they should be evaluated according to two hurdle rates. This avoids overinvesting in one and underinvesting in another. Also performance can be gauged relative to risk of each division.

13. A. run financial control, planning and treasury operations
    B. act as a bridge between operations and the investor community
    C. build and monitor value management capability throughout organization
    D. manage development and communication of corporate and financial strategy
    E. redesign corporate incentive systems around value

3

Fundamental Principles of Value Creation

1. C, D

2. D

3. B, D

4. C

5. B, C, D

6. A. install forward-looking performance measures
   B. align managers to value performance through incentives

7. A. earn returns in excess of opportunity cost of capital
   B. growth can create value only when excess returns are earned

C. select strategies that maximize the intrinsic present value of future economic profit or cash flow

D. market expectations might not be unbiased estimates of intrinsic value

E. shareholder returns depend on changes in their expectations of future performance rather than on actual performance

4

Metrics Mania: Surviving the Barrage of Value Metrics

1. A. cash flow drives share price performance
   B. short versus long-term tradeoffs are better understood economically
   C. economic measures uncover the sources of value

2. A. shareholder value
   B. intrinsic value
   C. value drivers
   D. incentives

3.

Approach	Pro	Con
TRS	Ultimate performance measure in the market	Managers assessed based on factors beyond their control
MVA	Financial market's view of future performance relative to how much is invested	Unable to assess how fast the firm accrues value or how much better the firm performs than the market
DCF	Future cash flows are evaluated at a rate commensurate with cash flow risk	Only an indicator of intrinsic value and must be compared with market expectations
ROIC	Critical component of operational assessment	Unable to detect whether enough return is being earned
Cost per unit	Factor in determining returns	Incomplete and misleading on its own

4. D

5. C, D

6. D

7. D

8. D

9. A. inconsistent valuation of inventory, depreciation across companies
   B. inflation
   C. cyclicality

D. irregular investment patterns

E. nonrecurring items.

10. D

11.

G\ROIC	14%	15%	16%
10%	5,714	6,667	7,500
12%	4,762	6,667	8,333
14%	0	6,667	12,500

14 percent ROIC is not sufficient to maintain increasingly higher levels of growth since economic profits are negative. At 16 percent, in excess of what the market rewards for the level of risk (i.e., 15% cost of capital), growth enhances value since economic profits are positive.

5

Cash Is King

---

1. C

2. A. growth is more important for high-spread than for low-spread companies
   B. at any level of growth higher spread leads to higher market value
   C. high discounted cash flow leads to high market value

3. A. when accounting changes (such as the switch to LIFO in deflationary times) result in cash flow increases, share value rises
   B. under pool-of-interests accounting even though goodwill is not deductible for tax purposes and so no cash flow effect, and thus no effect on shareholder expectations
   C. anecdotal evidence that pooling may create the opposite effect of market skepticism about the ability of the acquirer to create value

4. B, D

5. A. accounting methods on their own do not generate higher or
        lower share price differences
    B. when goodwill is not deductible there is a tax-related drop
        in cash flow and thus a lowering of share price
    C. choice of accounting methods may signal potential ability to
        generate future cash flow and thus affect share price

6. B

7. C

6

Making Value Happen

1. A. set targets
   B. align management processes
   C. structure incentives
   D. link value to culture

2.

	Traditional	*VBM*
Strengths	Nails down top-down governance issues through command and control Method-focused	Integrates top-down with bottom-up Realistic Decision-maker focused
Weaknesses	Esoteric, staff-based May ignore cultural and communications issues Narrow analytical focus Abstract	May become staff-based exercise Requires business-wide commitment, content and buy-in

3. A. metrics
   B. mindset

4. A. How does management balance long and short term?
   B. How and what opportunity cost of capital is included in the measurement of value?
   C. Are the metrics economic or accounting based?

5. A. Link quantitative targets to headline inspiration.
   B. Manage the business as a dynamic portfolio.
   C. Align organizational design and culture to the value imperative.
   D. Use value drivers for each business to develop insights into value creation.
   E. Manage business performance through value reviews.
   F. Incentivize people to add value and ferret out sources of nonvalue-adding activity.

6. For example:
   A. *Mission:* To help growing businesses obtain reliable and inexpensive power and gas.
   B. *Vision:* To create shareholder value by being the regional energy marketer of choice in offering price and volumetric risk management services to middle-tier end-users.

7. A. Reverse engineer financial market expectations in terms of your business.
   B. Use an industry fact base to found your arguments for value.
   C. Develop descriptions of role models from other and your own industry as a guide.

8. A. *Strategy:* Analyze corporate themes relative to current state-future state, industry guidelines and gaps among these.
   B. *Performance:* Relate corporate themes to hexagon restructuring opportunities.

C. *Growth:* Analyze current and future businesses against three ascending growth horizons.

9. For example (using the regional energy marketer above):

Theme	Your business	Industry leader
1. Industry shaper	Regionally, not nationally	National, but no local knowlede to preempt and reshape
2. Deal maker	Would love to, but no talent; could leverage regulated tariff-making skills	Eminent originator and structurer—customer pull organization
3. Scarce asset allocator	Leading cost minimizer in industry	Very efficient and activity-based coster
4. Skill replicator	Unsuccessful in repeated attempts	Incentivizes workforce to find cross-skill opportunities and markets
5. Performance manager	We still operate under seven platforms, have a bumbling shared business service operation, multiple faces to market	One face to the market, one process standard, one performance ethic, flexible realizations in multiple businesses
6. Talent agency	Who would want to work with/for us?	1 out of 50 applicants gets in; there are 2,000 applications a year for 100 jobs. Motto: Extraordinary pay for extraordinary results.
7. Growth asset allocator	Every business we own is declining or is increasing its share in buggy-whip markets.	New:old customer ratio is 2:1. 75% of new investment is in incubator activities. Company has real options philosophy to growing new businesses.

10. The value levers derive from EG's restructuring analysis along
     the lines of the hexagon. Completion of this matrix will provide
     a high-level guide for the portfolio of initiatives needed to im-
     prove value or stave off the deleterious effects of maintaining
     low or negative value businesses. Some examples motivate pos-
     sible answers. Answers can start out qualitatively, but should
     end up being quantitative.

Theme/lever	Investor communication	Internal improvements	Disposals	Growth opportunities	Financial engineering
1. Industry shaper	Invite bankers in to view latest Web-based load profile search en- gine. Investi- gate ideas for IPO.	Go to indus- try leader Franko Sys- tems and XrayConnect to put all businesses on common platform.			
2. Deal maker		$5 mm increase in sales staff will increase high margin deal contribution by $12 mm.	Develop expertise to manage energy impli- cations of customer disposals.		Match debt/equity to evolving asset earning capabilities.
3. Scarce asset allocator		Develop share services entity to begin out- sourcing of common transaction based functions.			
4. Skill replicator		Inventory skills, func- tions and tal- ent across each business. Identify over- laps, cross-			

Theme/lever	Investor communication	Internal improvements	Disposals	Growth opportunities	Financial engineering
		training, efficiency and growth opportunities.			
5. Performance manager			Identify top ten winners and losers. Eliminate losers. Cannibalize assets.		
6. Talent agency		Use new deal maker talent to recruit and develop local and new talent. Establish associate education programs with top universities.	Leverage good people out of bad businesses.		
7. Growth asset allocator				Establish regional incubator for energy solutions in alliance with local universities and wealth.	

11. For example, again following the regional energy marketer
    theme, here are some sample responses.

Profile/ Horizon	Expand degrees of freedom	Shape your destiny	Create future options
Types of businesses	Core energy user facilities management.	Energy end-user price and volumetric risk manager.	Bundle telecoms and branded facilities services on the Web.
Management imperative	Make extremely cost efficient—cannabilize and outsource.	Exercise market options to gain customer access and build internal portfolio management capability.	Use the Web to leap frog local competition, create excitement for stock value, align organization to customer needs, revamp information management operations.
Focus	Anchor operational efficiency and capital utilization for low margin product lines.	Swap real for virtual capital and focus on high margin product growth.	Develop portfolio of multiple exercise opportunities for multiple scenarios.

12. Another rendition of "for example" is displayed in the table fol-
    lowing. Although bordering on the abstract, this example can
    be tailored with instances of actual structures, company
    nomenclature, and the culture embedded in the vocabulary and
    syntax of day-to-day company living. This example derives from
    the regional energy marketer model developed previously
    whose core business was once heavily regulated by local
    authorities.

Orientation/ business	Core business	Shape your destiny
Reporting structures	Hierarchical with narrow reporting span	Flat with wide span
Decision authority	Allocated by capital/budget signing authority	Capital allocation
Key jobs	CEO, CFO, COO	Product leader, customer originator
Coordinating change	Top-down	Networked with communities of interest
Belief in potential value	Declining market therefore risky	Risky but feasible and necessary
Important success criteria	Cost minimization; hedge to protect the core	Customer value maximization: innovate to change the game
Leadership style	Command and control	Networked consensus with push-down responsibility

13. A. Aid in understanding how value is created or destroyed at any level in the business.

   B. Helps to prioritize where resources should be placed or removed to achieve target results.

   C. Able to align managers and employees around common understanding of value priorities.

14. Expanding on the energy marketer example, here are the beginnings of defining value drivers for a new growth business.

Principle	Driver	Explanation
Directly link to shareholder value creation	Additional revenue from high margin deals	Increases total revenue, which increases operating margin, which drives return on invested capital; ROIC in excess of opportunity cost of capital drives shareholder value up.
Cascade financial measures into underlying operational measures	Staff leverage	High leverage (low director to staff ratio) reduces operating costs, increases operating margin and so on.
Align operational measures with long-run growth	Bonus per staff	High bonuses retain higher margin employees with knowledge to innovate customer value deals as markets change in long run.

15. A. *Identification:* Create value trees to link operating elements to business value.

   B. *Prioritization:* Rank value sensitivities to value from highest to lowest.

   C. *Institutionalization:* Incorporate prioritized drivers into each business's balanced scorecard.

16. A. Clear value creation strategy.

   B. Clear link from targets to value drivers.

   C. Clearly understood calendar of performance reviews.

17. Generic issues and resolutions follow. It is important to tailor these to specific situations, businesses, and corporate cultures. Wording can mean everything in communicating performance expectations.

Issue	Resolution
Historically based targets do not reflect forward plan.	Review actual opportunities, industry analysis, stock analyst reports, and theoretical limits such as capacity utilization.
Stretch targets do not have clearly understood underlying motivation.	Use competitor benchmarking and benchmarking against comparable business units.
Driver reflects activity outside of management control—externalities.	Adjust targets to reflect the changing environment using predetermined rules.
Top-down and bottom-up targets do not agree.	Use an iterative negotiation between corporate center and business unit to resolve potential conflict where the corporate center is an equity analysis unit and the business unit supplies operating expertise.
Targets are not clearly understood between parties.	Use performance contracts to memorialize principles, measurements, milestones, and quantitative and qualitative goals over the performance period.

18. A. *What:* Use a customized scorecard that incorporates value metrics and key performance indicators from the value driver analysis.

    B. *When:* Use structured, repeating cycles of review that are part of management's agenda for the business that are coordinated with key events such as budgeting and individual performance reviews.

    C. *How:* Establish problem-solving tone with peer groups to encourage sharing of knowledge and forward vision.

19. A. *Financial:* Put a high percentage of total compensation at risk.

B. *Opportunity:* Rotate strong performers through responsibility spirals.

C. *Values and beliefs:* Emphasize satisfaction from acting according to business' brand.

20. A. Set base level of compensation higher than median companies.

    B. Base variable pay on performance formula.

    C. Do not cap bonuses. If necessary use bonus banks.

    D. Clearly draw the line concerning constraints (safety, ethical, etc.).

21. A. Top management commitment.

    B. Extensive and intensive business unit participation.

    C. Links to existing process and systems.

    D. Action-oriented, time-framed approach that is pragmatic, not abstract.

7

Mergers, Acquisitions, and Joint Ventures

1. The results of ex-ante and ex-post studies are summarized here:

Winners	Losers
Bigger overall value	Overoptimistic market potential
Low premium for acquisition	Overestimation of synergy
Acquirer is better run than acquired	Avoidance of major problems
Acquirer strength in core business	Overbidding in the heat of the deal
Link performance with incentives	Winner's curse: Why did everyone else drop out?
Focus on cash flow, not earnings	Poor postmerger integration
Take direct stake and repay within five years	Chasing good talent out
Fast improvement of underlying operations and preserve business continuity	Business disruption

2. A. Do your homework concerning the restructuring opportunities within which an M&A occur.

   B. Identify and screen M&A candidates.

   C. Assess high-potential candidates in depth.

   D. Contact, court, and negotiate candidates.

   E. Manage postmerger integration.

3. A. Leverage core business to access new customers.

   B. Capitalize on functional economies of scale.

   C. Align skills, knowledge, and technology transfer between companies.

4. A. The M&A will disrupt current business.

   B. Competitors will use M&A opportunity to woo customers away.

   C. Customers will bargain over price and quality during and after a merger.

5. A. Develop M&A database for periodic review.

   B. Apply knock-out criteria to filter candidates according to size, fit, strategy, markets, future value creation, and complementaries.

   C. Generate a short list of candidates for business unit/management review.

6.

Synergy	Characteristics
Universal	Available to nearly everyone (economies of scale, exploitable opportunities regarding pricing, overhead, waste)
Endemic	Available to only a few acquirers (brand investment, exclusive alliances)
Unique	Opportunities exploitable to only a few (intellectual property, geographical concessions)

7. A. The buyer or seller might not be willing.
   B. Play the drama of the deal.
   C. Use the negotiation to discover more about the other party's capabilities and intentions.
   D. Develop ways to handle potential stumbling blocks (earn-outs to bridge gaps, risk bearing, diversity in looking at future prospects, employee retention).
   E. Leverage both knowledge and dealing ability on the negotiating team.
   F. Keep to the logic of the deal.

8.

Issue	*Resolution*
Multiple business models confuse customers and employees about ability to generate value.	Define and develop business model during negotiation, ready for implementation upon signing.
Star performers will leave; top management will only agree abstractly about the way forward causing confusion and conflict.	Resolve uncertainty and conflict by including star performers in the process, maintain open and candid communications with all employees on frequent basis; move quickly to resolve uncertainty with practical action plans.
External entities (creditors, customers, regulators, etc.) may severely criticize or hold up M&A.	Maintain open communications with securities analysts, key customers.

9.

Characteristic	Merger/acquisition	Joint venture
Overlap	High levels to gain economies of scale in existing businesses	Complementary with little or no overlap; edging into new markets, geographies
Ownership split	Uneven	Even
Decision making	Centralized strategy	Autonomous and separate decision making
Time-frame	Perpetual	Contingent on meeting partners' goals

10. With the purchase method, the corresponding balance sheet items are added together at their fair market value appraisals. Debt is added to the financing balance to produce an overall new total book value. The difference between assets and financing is a new asset category called *goodwill,* the difference between the book value of the acquisition and the price paid.

Electric Car		M&M	
WC	30	Debt	35
NFA	105	Equity	110
Goodwill	10		
Total	145	Total	145

Under the purchase method, goodwill is amortized in the same way that fixed assets are depreciated. This will lower net income and cause lower tax liabilities.

Under the pooling method, the corresponding book values of the balance sheets are simply added together.

Electric Car		*M&M*	
WC	30	Debt	35
NFA	105	Equity	100
Total	135	Total	135

In this case, the equity drops from $110 + 20 = 130$ to 100 to accommodate the $35 million used to acquire the marketing firm. Herein lies the problems associated with pooling of interests with debt financing. Typically, pooling is only used when there is an all equity transfer of ownership. In that case, the balance sheet looks like this:

Electric Car		*M&M*	
WC	30		
NFA	105	Equity	135
Total	135	Total	135

Under this method, there is no amortization of differences between booked and market values of acquired assets so that reported net income will be higher than with purchase accounting.

8

Frameworks for Valuation

1. A. Free cash flow at the end of each of several forecasted periods.
   B. Discounts each cash flow by a rate of return commensurate with the riskiness of the cash flows.
   C. Sum up the discounted cash flows for an enterprise.

2. A. *Free cash flow* is "net operating profit less adjusted taxes," NOPLAT, minus net investment.
   B. *Net investment* is the amount of new capital and thus represents the growth in invested capital.
   C. The *investment rate* is the rate of NOPLAT that the firm decides to invest in new capital.

3. A. NOPLAT
   B. WACC
   C. Capital

The economic profit model of value discounts the period-by-period forecasted economic profit by the weighted-average, risk-adjusted, cost of capital. Economic profit is:

$$EP_t = N_t - w\, C_{t-1}$$

where N_t is end of period net operating profit less adjusted taxes, w is the weighted average cost of capital, and C_{t-1} is the beginning of period capital base used to generate operations. This measure can be restated multiplying N by C_{t-1}/C_{t-1} and rearranging to get

$$EP_t = (ROIC_{t,t-1} - w)C_{t-1}$$

where $ROIC_{t,\,t-1}$ is the end of period return on beginning of period capital.

4. To increase its value, a company, according to the free cash flow DCF model, would perform the following actions:
   - Increase capital only to increase NOPLAT by a higher than capital growth rate.
   - Decrease capital to lower the capital base, increase ROIC, but keeping NOPLAT from declining at the same or greater rate of capital decline.
   - Change capital to increase NOPLAT and ROIC, communicate this activity to the markets in the hopes of decreasing the weighted average, risk adjusted, cost of capital, WACC, thus overall increasing value.

5. This analysis follows ideas introduced as long ago as 1920 (GM residual income model) and more recently with Bennett Stewart's *Quest for Value* who labels the three firms as X, Y, Z.

   Consider three prototypical firms. Firm X's NOPLAT grows at a 10 percent rate per year. It plows back 100 percent of NOPLAT per year so that its capital growth is 10 percent per year, just like NOPLAT's growth. The increase in NOPLAT per increase in capital is a return of 10 percent on a NOPLAT base of $1,000.

   Then there is firm Y whose NOPLAT growth on $1,000 is also 10 percent. However, firm Y plows back 80 percent of its NOPLAT into capital. Its rate of return is higher at 12.5 percent. Firm Y grows NOPLAT at the same rate as firm X, but uses less capital to do so; firm Y should be more profitable. Firm Y also generates more *free cash flow,* as measured by NOPLAT – Investment.

Finally there is firm Z. This firm also earns a base NOPLAT of $1,000. But this firm, unlike X or Y invests 200 percent of NOPLAT in the capital base. Firm Z generates a negative free cash flow of $1,000 – 2 × 1,000 = –$1,000. This means that any dividends or interest and principal to be paid out must be financed each year. How can such a firm stay alive? Bankers are now asked to rank the three firms in terms of free cash flow.

	X	Y	Z
ROIC	10.0%	12.5%	12.5%
WACC	10.0%	10.0%	10.0%
Growth	10.0%	10.0%	25.0%
Investment rate	100.0%	80.0%	200.0%
NOPLAT	1,000	1,000	1,000
Net investment	1,000	800	2,000
Free cash flow	—	200	(1,000)
NOPLAT increase	100.00	100.00	250.00
ROIC on new capital	10.0%	12.5%	12.5%
EP on new capital	0	20	50

Most bankers might prefer Firm Y, with firm X second, and firm Z to be bankrupted. Let's further suppose that all three firms are perceived by the markets to have the same expected level of risk and earn a 10 percent cost of capital. Let firm Z earn the same ROIC as Y (i.e., 12.5%).

Firm Z grows more rapidly than X or Y at 25 percent. (12.5% × 200% = ROIC × Investment/NOPLAT). For firm Z, the increase in NOPLAT is really at the 25 percent rate, so that an extra 250 is earned on an extra $2,000 of capital (12.5% return). Thus firm Z's aggressive capital spending campaign will fuel even higher levels of NOPLAT growth. Profitability is high, just like firm Y. But so is the firm's growth and the growth in NOPLAT, something that firm Y does not achieve.

Which firm earns more value added? The clear winner is firm Z. The curve ball is firm Z's willingness to fuel higher NOPLAT with additions to capacity, the long run and fundamental fix.

To summarize: Firm X generates 0 free cash flow, by investing all of its earnings in a mediocre operation resulting in no value added. Firm Y generates part of its earnings in a mediocre enterprise, keeps some free cash flow and does add some value. Firm Z generates negative free cash flow by investing more than its earnings in a superior enterprise and thereby adds much more value than either X or Y. Z plans to pump more money into excellent projects on a regular, predictable basis.

6. The Modigliani-Miller valuation formula is particularly useful in demonstrating the sources of value in a firm in a simplified way. The basic idea is to value the assets in place plus growth opportunities. The value of assets in place is the no-growth NOPLAT discounted by WACC in perpetuity:

$$V_{inplace} = \frac{NOPLAT}{WACC}$$

A. For a firm with \$100 in NOPLAT and a weighted average cost of capital of 10 percent, value of assets in place is:

$$V_{inplace} = \frac{NOPLAT}{WACC} = \frac{100}{0.1} = 1000$$

B. The value of future growth opportunities is:

$$V_{growth} = Kn(NOPLAT)\left[\frac{(ROIC - WACC)}{WACC(1 + WACC)}\right]$$

where K is the percent of NOPLAT invested for growth projects, n is the number of years during which the firm expects to invest in new projects and earn the ROIC at the WACC rate of return. In the formula, $Kn(NOPLAT)(ROIC - WACC)/WACC$ is the n year present value economic profit earned on the investment capital in growth projects, beginning one year from the date of the valuation. The term $1/(1 + WACC)$ discounts the PV of future economic growth profits back to the present. Suppose that the firm has a five-year window for competitive position, with an ROIC of 20 percent and a rate of reinvestment K of 200 percent. The value of growth opportunities is then:

$$V_{growth} = Kn(NOPLAT)\left[\frac{(ROIC - WACC)}{WACC(1+WACC)}\right]$$

$$= (2)(5)(100)\left\{\frac{[0.2-0.1]}{[.1(1.1)]}\right\} = 909$$

C. The total value of the firm is then:

$$V = V_{in\ place} + V_{growth} = 1000 + 909 = 1,909$$

Changes in the competitive window, the rate of reinvestment, the economic profit spread, and the base level of initiating earnings all contribute in consistent ways to build a story of firm value.

7. The steps in a valuation include:

   A. *Analyze historical performance.* Gather together a set of appropriate comparable firms. Calculate NOPLAT, invested capital, and value drivers. Integrate into this analysis a perspective that includes a business system, strategic, and industry analysis.

   B. *Forecast performance.* Use the current industry and firm strategic position construct probable scenarios for various future competitive positions. Forecast line items. Check for completeness, consistency, and parsimony.

   C. *Estimate the cost of capital.* Develop target market value weights for each capital category. Estimate the costs of equity and non-equity financing with careful attention to using as objective a set of criteria and modeling as possible.

D. *Estimate continuing value.* Consider the explicit forecast horizon, appropriate valuation techniques, and key parameters. Discount to the present using the cost of capital.

E. *Calculate and interpret results.* Finish the valuation by tying together the explicit forecast and continuing value discounts. Interpret results within the strategic change envisioned for the firm and the concomitant decisions that need to be taken to maximize value.

9

Analyzing Historical Performance

1. A. *Starting points:* Return on invested capital (ROIC) and the weighted average cost of capital (WACC). (ROIC measures the firm's ability to yield net results to all stakeholders, irrespective of financing arrangements. The minimum return investors require to be compensated for their perception of risk in the firm's business operations is measured by WACC. The difference between ROIC and WACC measures the per currency unit of capital results of a firm's periodic operations. This spread is the economic profit yield of the firm. When multiplied by the amount of beginning (or average) capital, economic profit is measured.

   B. *Ultimate goals:* To help managers and investors understand when the firm is or is not value creating. (Thus the analysis is not simply a calculation of ROIC or WACC measures, but their combination in an economic profit calculation. When ROIC exceeds WACC, managers are returning positive economic profits. When ROIC equals or falls short of investors' risk adjusted expectations, there are economic losses. Economic profit adds market value, creates an excess demand for the company's stocks, and can lower WACC, producing even higher expectations of value creation.)

2. The determinants of ROIC are:

A. Using the "Dupont" system, ROIC, like any ratio, can be decomposed into several underlying components. The result is a tree of ROIC determinants. At the top is ROIC. At the second level are pretax ROIC and EBIT Cash Tax Rate (CTR). On the next level are asset turnover into sales and operating income margin. Further levels can be constructed by decomposing operating income margin and asset to sales turns into their components, and so on.

ROIC is first stripped of tax considerations into a pretax ROIC:

$$\text{Pretax ROIC} = \frac{\text{ROIC}}{(1 - \text{EBIT cash tax rate})}$$

where, from the NOPLAT statement, EBIT Cash Tax Rate (CTR) equals:

$$\text{CTR} = \frac{(\text{Taxes on EBIT} + \text{Change in deferred taxes})}{\text{EBIT}}$$

B. Tax considerations in this analysis are relegated to a different category than are operational experiences. Tax rates, and the extent to which they can be effectively managed, must be compared across firms in the firm's industry universe.

Nontax operating return, pretax ROIC can be further decomposed into

$$\text{Pretax ROIC} = \left(\frac{\text{EBIT}}{\text{Sales}}\right) \times \left(\frac{\text{Sales}}{\text{Invested capital}}\right)$$

EBIT/sales, the operating margin or operating return on sales, measures the way sales converts into after expenses income. Within-period operating efficiency is measured by this ratio. Sales/invested capital measures how effective capital is in producing sales. More sales for every dollar of long run operating capital shows an effective use of capital. More asset turns coupled with a highly efficient operation, in terms of a high operating margin, produces high levels of ROIC for a given CTR. In turn, a poor ROIC can be produced by three significant factors: high tax rates, inefficient operations, and ineffective capital.

EBIT/sales in turn can be decomposed into the various cost components of operating income:

$$\frac{EBIT}{Sales} = 1 - \frac{Expense}{Sales}$$

where

$$\frac{Expense}{Sales} = \frac{COGS}{Sales} + \frac{SG\&A}{Sales} + \frac{Dep}{Sales}$$

where COGS is cost of goods sold, SG&A is sales, general and administrative expenses, and Dep is depreciation. While depreciation is a noncash expense, it does attempt to represent the user cost of expended capital during the period of operation. In this sense, capital is an unexpended cost to be maintained within the context of the going concern of the perpetual firm.

C. Capital effectiveness, measured by sales/invested capital can also be decomposed:

$$\frac{Sales}{Capital} = \frac{1}{\left(\dfrac{WC}{Sales} + \dfrac{NFA}{Sales} + \dfrac{OA}{Sales} \right)}$$

where WC is working capital, NFA is net fixed assets, and OA is other assets. Lower values of these ratios indicated increased effectiveness of the components of the invested capital portfolio as they contribute to sales.

3. Here is the beginning of the historical analysis:

	1998	1999
Invested Capital Statement		
Working capital	154	117
Long term assets	1,430	1,411
Operating invested capital	1,584	1,528
Net investment		(56)
Debt	507	447
Equity	1,077	1,081
NOPLAT Statement		
Sales	4,056	4,192
Operating expenses	(3,307)	(3,408)
General expenses	(562)	(528)
Depreciation	(139)	(136)
EBIT	48	120
Taxes on EBIT	(31)	(53)
Change in deferred taxes	(29)	(20)
NOPLAT	(12)	47
Provision for income taxes	(7)	41
Tax shield on interest expense	25	13
Tax on investment income	(3)	(3)
Tax on non-operating income	16	2
Taxes on EBIT	31	53

Invested capital has operating and financing sides. On the operating side is operating working capital and long-run operating capital net of accumulated depreciation. Operating working capital is operating current assets (not marketable securities) net of non-interest bearing current liabilities (NIBCLs). On the financing side is currently due debt plus long run debt. The rest is equity, computed as a residual between invested capital and debt. This equity amount includes total booked equity plus deferred taxes as an equity equivalent.

The NOPLAT statement itself is simple: sales minus operating costs minus operating taxes. The accounting statement of net income provides a total provision for income taxes. This provision includes tax deductions for interest payments and taxes and deductions for non-operating income. Adjusting for these items we get taxes on EBIT. One further adjustment is required due to the mismatching of accounting tax treatments and the actual treatment due to accelerated depreciation schemes for tax deductibility of depreciation. This last adjustment is contained in the changes to the virtual perpetual loan the tax authorities give a firm—deferred taxes.

4. The net income statement and its reconciliation to NOPLAT:

	1998	1999
Net Income Statement		
Sales	4,056	4,192
Operating expenses	(3,307)	(3,408)
General expenses	(562)	(528)
Depreciation	(139)	(136)
EBIT	48	120
Investment income	5	6
Investment expense	(39)	(30)
Miscellaneous, net	(25)	(4)
Earnings before taxes	(11)	92
Income taxes	7	(41)
Net income (before extra items)	(4)	51
Tax Rate	64%	45%
Reconciliation to Net Income Statement		
Net income	(4)	51
Add: Increase in deferred taxes	(29)	(20)
Adjusted net income	(33)	31
Add: Interest expense after tax	14	17
Income available to investors	(19)	48
Less: Interest income after tax	(2)	(3)
Less: Non-operating income after tax	9	2
NOPLAT	(12)	47

The primary utility of this exercise is to be sure that the NOPLAT statement is complete and consistent with the data. It is complete because all of the relevant cost, tax, and operating data included in the accounting net income statement is also included for operations in the NOPLAT statement. It is consistent with the net income statement through the reconciliation process. That process primarily derives from the cash tax treatment.

5. Here is the value driver tree:

	1998	1999
ROIC Tree		
ROIC	−0.7%	3.0%
= (1 − EBIT cash tax rate)	−24.1%	38.8%
× Pretax ROIC	3.0%	7.9%
= EBIT/Sales	1.2%	2.9%
× Sales/Invested capital	2.56	2.74
EBIT/Sales = 1 − (Operating expenses/Sales	81.5%	81.3%
+ General expenses/Sales	13.9%	12.6%
+ Depreciation/Sales)	3.4%	3.2%
Sales/Invested capital		
= 1/(Operating working capital/Sales	3.8%	2.8%
+ Long term operating assets/Sales)	35.3%	33.7%

The ROIC in 1998 is near zero and negative. The tree shows that the low pretax ROIC derives both from a low operating margin of 1.2 percent and an ineffective capital usage of $2.56 sales for every $1 of capital invested in operations. The low operating margin derives from high expense-to-sales ratios. The low capital effectiveness derives from high capital to sales ratios.

The situation improves from 1998 to 1999 with an improvement in ROIC to 7 percent. This is due both to improvements in operations (lower costs, increased operational efficiency) and in capital utilization (less assets relative to sales).

6. The free cash flow statement.
    Free cash flow is the difference between NOPLAT and net investment. Net investment in turn is the gross investment net of depreciation. Investment derives from changes in operating working capital and capital expenditures. Total cash flow available to investors includes free cash flow from operations plus non-operating income.

	1999
Free Cash Flow Statement	
NOPLAT	47
Depreciation	136
Gross cash flow	183
Increase in operating working capital	(37)
Capital expenditures	117
Gross investment	80
Free cash flow	103
Non-operating cash flow	2
Cash flow available to investors	105

7. Economic profit is the difference between operating earnings, NOPLAT, and the return expected by investors for the level of risk perceived.

	1999
Economic Profit	
NOPLAT	47
Capital charge	(170.1)
Economic Profit	(123.6)

The capital charge is the 11.1 percent weighted average cost of capital times the amount of capital. This is obviously a period in the life of the firm that is value detracting.

Note: Comparison between the free cash flow and economic profit statements

Both measures begin with NOPLAT, operating earnings derived by using the long-run operating capital base. Free cash flow measures the residual cash from operations after sales- or cost-driven increases in capital have been deducted from operating earnings. On the other hand, economic profit measures the residual value from operations after a risk adjusted return has been deducted from operating earnings.

Free cash flow is useful for determining the funds use and need during a period's operations. Economic profit is useful for determining the ability of a period's operations to contribute to the increase or decrease in the overall value of the enterprise. From the definition of economic profit:

$$\text{Economic profit} = \text{NOPLAT} - \text{WACC} \times \text{Invested capital}$$

Dividing, then multiplying both sides by invested capital gives us the useful expression:

$$\text{Economic profit} = (\text{ROIC} - \text{WACC}) \times \text{Invested capital}$$

Economic profit is determined by the spread between operating results, ROIC, and investors' expectations of return, WACC, times the amount of capital employed. Increases in operating efficiency and capital effectiveness will increase ROIC, which in turn increases the spread and thus economic profit. At a given spread, no further risk to investors, and no further improvement in operating returns, an increase in capital will also increase economic profit.

For Freight Ways, free cash flow is positive. This might make bondholders happy, since their cash sensitive position would require prompt and complete contractual payments on outstanding debt. However, for all of the excess cash produced, there is not enough operating income to pay the investors what they would expect given their perceptions of risk. Freight Ways is value detracting, perhaps, because it does not have profitable opportunities in which to invest.

10

Estimating the Cost of Capital

1. Be comprised of a weighted average of the costs of all sources of financial capital.

   With market value weights for each element (book values do not represent the financial economic claim to the component's cash flows).

   A. Be computed on after-tax basis (free cash flow is after-tax).

   B. Use nominal rates of return (real returns + expected inflation).

   C. Reflect the systematic riskiness of cash flows.

   D. Reflect the time-varying nature of interest rates and risk premia (in other words, different rates at different future dates).

2. The steps needed to estimate the weighted-average cost of capital are:

   A. Establish target market value weights for each capital layer.

   B. Estimate the opportunity cost of non-equity financing on an after-tax basis.

   C. Estimate the opportunity cost of equity financing.

3. Three approaches are:

   A. Estimate current market value of the capital structure of the company.

B. Review capital structure of comparable companies.

C. Review management's approach to financing and its implications for a target capital structure.

4. Bond A: 100 percent repayment at the end of year 2. Coupon
interest cash flow is coupon rate × face value = 0.1 × 1,000 =
100 (negative to the issuer). Internal rate of return is the rate
that equates the year 0 cash flow to the present value of the
bond, that is, find the yield, y, such that:

$$1000 = \frac{-100}{(1+y)^1} + \frac{-1100}{(1+y)^2}$$

Year	0	1	2
Interest		−100	−100
Principal	+1,000		−1,000
Net cash flow	+1,000	−100	−1,100
Internal rate of return	10%		

For Bond B: 50 percent repayment in year 1, with the remainder
(50%) in year 2. Interest in year 2 has two components: −100
coupon interest payable and +50 escrow interest receivable
from the sinking fund.

Year	0	1	2
Interest		−100	−50
Principal	+1,000	−500	−500
Net cash flow	+1,000	−600	−550
Internal rate of return	10%		

Will both bonds sell for that same price? Not necessarily. The sinking fund bond (B) might be sold for a premium (more than face value) to reflect reduced risk (yield < coupon rate) of repayment to investors (or at a lower coupon rate to sell at par = face value). Also escrow interest might be less than the coupon rate. The cost of the capital of the two bonds is (nominally) the internal rate of return associated with the bonds' cash flows or 10 percent pretax.

5. Only net interest income is taxable; principal is not. The after-tax cost of bond A capital is exactly $10\% \times (1 - 0.4) = 6\%$, since interest paid is deductible in each of the two repayment periods. In spite of the lump-sum pay-out at the end of year 2, bond A costs less (yields less to investors) because most of the cash flow out is deferred to the end of year two.

Bond A Post-Tax			
Face	1,000		
Coupon	10%		
Tax rate	40%		
		Year	
	0	**1**	**2**
Interest received			
Interest paid		−100	−100
Tax	0	40	40
Principal	1,000		−1,000
Cash flow	1,000	−60	−1,060
Yield	6%		

The after-tax cost of bond B reflects a more complex average of the repayment cash flow since it is now spread more evenly across the two repayment periods. Investors get their cash sooner, but issuers get to pay earlier than with bond A.

Bond B Post-Tax			
Face	1,000		
Coupon	10%		
Tax rate	40%		
		Year	
	0	*1*	*2*
Interest received			50
Interest paid		−100	−100
Tax	0	40	20
Principal	1,000	−500	−500
Cash flow	1,000	−560	−580
Yield	9%		

A lesson worth heeding: Compute cash flows on an after-tax basis, then compute the after-tax yield to approximate the cost of capital for the instrument.

7. Step 1 results in:

Target debt percent	0%	50%	75%
Target equity percent	100%	50%	25%
Target growth	5%	5%	5%
Target ROIC	20%	20%	20%
Face value of debt	0	5,000	7,500
Book value: Equity	10,000	5,000	2,500
Book value: Assets	10,000	10,000	10,000
Tax rate	40%	40%	40%
Cost of debt	10%	15%	20%
Unlevered beta	0.8	0.8	0.8
Levered beta	0.8	1.28	2.24
Risk-free rate	7.00%	7.00%	7.00%
Market premium	6.00%	6.00%	6.00%
Cost of equity	11.80%	14.68%	20.44%
WACC	11.80%	11.84%	14.11%
NOI	5,300	5,300	5,300
Tax	−2,120	−2,120	−2,120
NOPLAT	3,180	3,180	3,180
Net investment	−795	−795	−795
Free cash flow	2,385	2,385	2,385
Value of assets	35,074	34,868	26,180

Replacing the book value of assets with the discounted cash flow value results in the first iteration of step 2:

Target debt percent	0%	50%	50%
Target equity percent	100%	50%	25%
Target growth	5%	5%	5%
Target ROIC	20%	20%	20%
Face value of debt	0	5,000	7,500
Book value: Equity	35,074	29,868	18,680
Market value: Assets	35,074	34,868	26,180
Tax rate	40%	40%	40%
Cost of debt	10%	15%	20%
Unlevered beta	0.8	0.8	0.8
Levered Beta	0.8	0.880352	0.992719
Risk-free rate	7.00%	7.00%	7.00%
Market premium	6.00%	6.00%	6.00%
Cost of equity	11.80%	12.28%	12.96%
WACC	11.80%	11.81%	12.68%
NOI	5,300	5,300	5,300
Tax	−2,120	−2,120	−2,120
NOPLAT	3,180	3,180	3,180
Net investment	−795	−795	−795
Free cash flow	2,385	2,385	2,385
Value of assets	35,074	35,014	31,045

After two more iterations, WACC does not change significantly (to two decimal places of precision as specified above):

Target debt percent	0%	50%	50%
Target equity percent	100%	50%	25%
Target growth	5%	5%	5%
Target ROIC	20%	20%	20%
Face value of debt	0	5,000	7,500
Book value: Equity	35,074	30,015	24,170
Market value: Assets	35,074	35,015	31,670
Tax rate	40%	40%	40%
Cost of debt	10%	15%	20%
Unlevered beta	0.8	0.8	0.8
Levered beta	0.8	0.879961	0.948942
Risk-free rate	7.00%	7.00%	7.00%
Market premium	6.00%	6.00%	6.00%
Cost of equity	11.80%	12.28%	12.69%
WACC	11.80%	11.81%	12.53%
NOI	5,300	5,300	5,300
Tax	−2,120	−2,120	−2,120
NOPLAT	3,180	3,180	3,180
Net investment	−795	−795	−795
Free cash flow	2,385	2,385	2,385
Value of assets	35,074	35,015	31,676

11

Forecasting Performance

1. Five steps include:
   A. Determine length and level of forecast detail. Most analysts use stages of growth: near, intermediate, and far.
   B. Develop a strategy story that links to performance. This is typically a "Porter" style industry analysis with strengths, weaknesses, threats, and opportunities internally. A balanced score card should map future strategic realizations to performance forecast scenarios.
   C. Translate strategy into financial forecasts: income statement, balance sheet, free cash flow, and value drivers.
   D. Develop performance scenarios that can be simulated.
   E. Check forecasts for consistency, completeness, and alignment with strategy.

2. The evaluation of strategic position itself asks at least the following six questions:
   A. *Buyers:* Who are they? What are their preferences? What pricing and product practices will meet their expectations? Increasing ROIC derives from enhanced revenues, less charge backs for returned and poor quality product, and reasonably designed customer satisfaction.

B. *Sellers:* Again, who are they? How can they best serve the firm in its mission to serve the firm's customers and clients? Increasing ROIC and lower WACC derives from lower, efficient, and more productive and effective cost and asset structures. Lower WACC derives from higher financial quality, lower perceived risks from financial capital suppliers, due to lower perceived volatility and greater ability to manage uncertainty.

C. *Technology:* What is the cycle of innovation in the industry, the rate of turnover of generations of capital, the ability of the firm to innovate in well-planned research and development? Higher ROIC and lower WACC derive from the firm's short run ability to react to incursions in its technological base and obsolescence as technology turns over from generation to generation. More R&D means lower-cost production and products that meet the changing expectations of customers.

D. *Government:* What are the cycles of regulation, deregulation, and re-regulation in the industry? How do these regulatory movements impact production, choice of capital, choice of where to raise capital, vendor quality, liability with stakeholders, and choice of customer market segments? Each of these items impacts: (1) the ability of the firm to influence operating margins, (2) investors to post a level of perceived risk in the cost of capital, and (3) find and retain customers with appropriate pricing practices.

E. *New entrants:* What are the threats, barriers to entry, ability to re-engineer new technology, and entrepreneurial availability in the industry? This question directly impacts the ability of the firm to maintain its positive ROIC over WACC, in other words, its quasi-monopolistic position. Relatively low barriers to entry can be produced by skewed regulatory systems, for example, that favor small over larger businesses. In the long run, a financial forecast must recognize the positive probability of handing over the long-run asset base produced by current thinking and technology to new entrants. In this case, ROIC will tend to WACC and even fall below

WACC at which point the firm goes out of its current business and into another.

F. *Substitute products/services:* A similar set of questions and logic obtains for this inquiry as for new entrants. As IBM found out with its RISC technology, even a competing product can be found within a firm's multidivisional structure.

High value added occurs with high ROIC and low WACC. High ROIC occurs with higher operational efficiency (*seller*), more effective capital (*seller, technology*), achieving lower costs than the competition (*substitute products, new entrants*), and providing superior value to the customer (*buyer*).

3. *Customer segmentation* estimates the potential market share, growth of sales, and ability to maintain and grow markets. The company segments customers and products by various attributes, then associates those attributes with the various core competencies of the firm to provide goods and services.

Business system analysis provides the core competencies and abilities of the firm to meet customer expectations. Issues such as time-to-market, access to sources of material and labor, cycle time, packaging, and distribution channels are combined to highlight the competitive advantages and disadvantages the firm possesses in its industry.

Industry structure provides insight into the cycle of feed forward and feedback networks at work in the industry analysis of buyer, seller, government, technology, new entrants, and substitute product attributes. This component of the analysis provides the dynamic interrelationships among various industry players.

4. Three scenarios are possible with this data: The construction of scenarios will include a sales forecast growth rate, expense ratio structure, sales-to-asset structure and capital growth rate in the long run.

A. Status Quo (SQ) industry remains as it has over the past 5 years, and IMT maintains its market share, technological and global competitiveness: The goal is to maintain operational efficiency and capital effectiveness and improve overhead expense structures in an arena of positive tax rates. Operating expense/sales of 74 percent in perpetuity, SG&A/sales of 16 percent, 3 years of sales growth at 20 percent per year, historical working capital, and long run capital to sales relationships.

B. Aggressive (AG) IMT introduces significant changes and increases to its product line and ability to meet technological change in the industry: The goal is to improve all expense structures at high levels of sales growth over the near term. Operating expense/sales of 74 percent, 73 percent, 73 percent for 3 years, SG&A/sales of 16 percent, 3 years of sales growth of 40 percent, reflecting the special ability of this firm to outperform the economy.

C. Conservative (CO) IMT is barely able to hold its own in the global arena of faster paced technological change and customer demands: The goal is to maintain historical sales, operating and general expense structures. Operating expense/sales of 74 percent in perpetuity, SG&A/sales of 19 percent, 3 years of sales growth at 20 percent per year.

The SQ scenario is management's best guess for continued health of the firm. It reflects the status quo structures of the firm to innovate and improve—not remain in a holding position. On the other hand, the CO scenario is maintenance of past operating results and represents, for management and management's communication to the investment community, the effects of a non-innovative scenario. Finally, the AG scenario is the one that management could hope for if all conditions are right, including those not in management's power. Implicit in the success that an AG scenario represents is management's willingness to put resources to value-adding activities when they occur, either by design, or as a result of market conditions.

5.

Driver	A: Low growth CO	B: Medium growth SQ	C: High growth AG
Operating expenses/sales	74%	74%	74%,73%,73%
SGA/sales	19%	16%	16%
Growth	20%	20%	40%
Other	Ratios constant	Ratios constant	Ratios constant

Forecasts for the three scenarios follow. In each there are four columns. The first is the last available historical year, 1999, followed by, in this case, three forecast years, 2000, 2001, 2002. A simplified invested capital statement precedes the calculate of the forecasted net investment, or change in invested capital useful in the subsequent free cash flow calculation. Next comes the NOPLAT statement. Items in boxes are input to the forecasting process. Finally, ratios, forecasted and derived, and a free cash flow forecast are provided.

Since this is a sales driven forecast, historical sales starts the forecast. Sales growth is projected over the forecast period. Next year's sales is equal to this year's, times one, plus the projected growth rate for sales over the period. This year's expenses equal the year's forecasted sales times the appropriate forecasted expense ratio. Similarly, working capital and long run asset ratios are used to project forecasted invested capital items from this year's forecasted sales.

Forecasts of debt to invested capital ratios and projected debt interest rates will be used in cost of capital and economic profit studies in the next chapter.

Tax rate forecasts are used both for cost of capital studies and the forecast of NOPLAT. Forecasted changes in deferred taxes to sales are used in the NOPLAT calculation.

Status Quo	H 1999	F 2000	F 2001	F 2002
WC	193.000	231.525	277.830	333.396
NFAOA	246.000	296.352	355.622	426.747
IC	439.000	527.877	633.452	760.143
Net Investment		88.877	105.575	126.690
Debt	314.000	343.120	411.744	494.093
Equity	125.000	184.757	221.708	266.050
Sales growth		20.00%	20.00%	20.00%
Net sales	1,029.000	1,234.800	1,481.760	1,778.112
Operating expenses		(917.456)	(1,100.948)	(1,321.137)
SG&A		(197.568)	(237.082)	(284.498)
Depreciation		(30.870)	(37.044)	(44.453)
Operating income		88.906	106.687	128.024
Taxes on EBIT		(35.562)	(42.675)	(51.210)
Change in deferred tax		2.396	2.875	3.450
NOPLAT		55.739	66.887	80.264
ROIC		10.56%	10.56%	10.56%
D/IC		65.00%	65.00%	65.00%
Eq/IC		35.00%	35.00%	35.00%
Tax rate	−21.62%	40.00%	40.00%	40.00%
Interest rate	5.10%	6.00%	7.00%	7.00%
Growth (investment/capital)		20.25%	20.00%	20.00%
Investment rate (Gwh/ROIC)		191.73%	189.41%	189.41%
EBIT/sales		7.2000%	7.2000%	7.2000%
Sales/IC		2.3392	2.3392	2.3392
WC/sales	18.7561%	18.7500%	18.7500%	18.7500%
NFAOA/sales	23.9067%	24.0000%	24.0000%	24.0000%
Operating expenses/ sales	74.3440%	74.3000%	74.3000%	74.3000%
SG&A/sales	18.5617%	16.0000%	16.0000%	16.0000%
Depreciation/sales	2.5267%	2.5000%	2.5000%	2.5000%
Chg def'd tx/sales	0.194%	0.194%	0.194%	0.194%
Free cash flow		(33.138)	(38.689)	(46.427)

A number of derived results can attest to the effect of these particular scenarios on the firm. ROIC is a constant 10.56 percent, below the 1999 high of 13.5 percent, due primarily to the positive 40 percent tax rate. However, EBIT to Sales is vastly improved from 4.6 percent to 7.2 percent, not on the backs of line workers directly involved with producing revenues, but on low quality and value detracting overhead activities with a lower general expense-to-sales ratio. Caution must be exercised in achieving the low general expense ratio of 16 percent in that truly value-detracting activities be identified and culled from the high-quality, revenue, and productivity enhancing overheads (see page 173).

The AG scenario forecasts higher ROIC, better operations and no change in effective use of capital. Free cash flow is increasingly negative (see page 174).

The CO scenario posts the poorest performance, with low ROIC, operations, and capital ratios. Capital is required as sales rise by 20 percent per year. Cash flow is negative with net investment exceeding NOPLAT.

Aggressive	H 1999	F 2000	F 2001	F 2002
WC	193.000	270.113	378.158	529.421
NFAOA	246.000	345.744	484.042	677.658
IC	439.000	615.857	862.199	1,207.079
Net Investment		176.857	246.343	344.880
Debt	314.000	400.307	560.429	784.601
Equity	125.000	215.550	301.770	422.478
Sales growth		40.00%	40.00%	40.00%
Net sales	1,029.000	1,440.600	2,016.840	2,823.576
Operating expenses		(1,066.044)	(1,472.293)	(2,061.210)
SG&A		(230.496)	(322.694)	(451.772)
Depreciation		(36.015)	(50.421)	(70.589)
Operating income		108.045	171.431	240.004
Taxes on EBIT		(43.218)	(68.573)	(96.002)
Change in deferred tax		2.795	3.913	5.478
NOPLAT		67.622	106.772	149.480
ROIC		10.98%	12.38%	12.38%
D/IC		65.00%	65.00%	65.00%
Eq/IC		35.00%	35.00%	35.00%
Tax rate	−21.62%	40.00%	40.00%	40.00%
Interest rate	5.10%	6.00%	7.00%	7.00%
Growth (investment/ capital)		40.29%	40.00%	40.00%
Investment rate (Gwh/ROIC)		366.90%	323.01%	323.01%
EBIT/sales		7.5000%	8.5000%	8.5000%
Sales/IC		2.3392	2.3392	2.3392
WC/sales	18.7561%	18.7500%	18.7500%	18.7500%
NFAOA/sales	23.9067%	24.0000%	24.0000%	24.0000%
Operating expenses/sales	74.3440%	74.0000%	73.0000%	73.0000%
SG&A/sales	18.5617%	16.0000%	16.0000%	16.0000%
Depreciation/sales	2.5267%	2.5000%	2.5000%	2.5000%
Change in deferred tax/sales	0.194%	0.194%	0.194%	0.194%
Free cash flow		(109.235)	(139.571)	(195.400)

Conservative	H 1999	F 2000	F 2001	F 2002
WC	193.000	231.525	277.830	333.396
NFAOA	246.000	296.352	355.622	426.747
IC	439.000	527.877	633.452	760.143
Net Investment		88.877	105.575	126.690
Debt	314.000	343.120	411.744	494.093
Equity	125.000	184.757	221.708	266.050
Sales growth		20.00%	20.00%	20.00%
Net sales	1,029.000	1,234.800	1,481.760	1,778.112
Operating expenses		(926.100)	(1,111.320)	(1,333.584)
SG&A		(229.673)	(275.607)	(330.729)
Depreciation		(31.200)	(37.440)	(44.928)
Operating income		47.828	57.393	68.872
Taxes on EBIT		(19.131)	(22.957)	(27.549)
Change in deferred tax		2.396	2.875	3.450
NOPLAT		31.092	37.310	44.773
ROIC		5.89%	5.89%	5.89%
D/IC		65.00%	65.00%	65.00%
Eq/IC		35.00%	35.00%	35.00%
Tax rate	−21.62%	40.00%	40.00%	40.00%
Interest rate	5.10%	6.00%	7.00%	7.00%
Growth (investment/capital)		20.25%	20.00%	20.00%
Investment rate (Gwh/ROIC)		343.72%	339.56%	339.56%
EBIT/sales		3.8733%	3.8733%	3.8733%
Sales/IC		2.3392	2.3392	2.3392
WC/sales	18.7561%	18.7500%	18.7500%	18.7500%
NFAOA/sales	23.9067%	24.0000%	24.0000%	24.0000%
Operating expenses/sales	74.3440%	75.0000%	75.0000%	75.0000%
SG&A/sales	18.5617%	18.6000%	18.6000%	18.6000%
Depreciation/sales	2.5267%	2.5267%	2.5267%	2.5267%
Change in deferred tax/sales	0.194%	0.194%	0.194%	0.194%
Free cash flow		(57.785)	(68.265)	(81.918)

12

Estimating Continuing Value

1. There are four steps that lead to a consistent and complete forecast of continuing value:

   A. *Select an appropriate technique:* An analyst can either produce a 75-year forecast (growing perpetuity effectively), use a growing free cash flow perpetuity, or a value-driver derivation of a growing free cash flow perpetuity. All three techniques produce the same results when the same underlying assumptions about capital growth, return on new investment, and initial NOPLAT or FCF conditions.

   B. *Decide on a horizon for the explicit forecast period:* If a 75-plus year horizon is used, then simply forecast the first year's free cash flow (or economic profit plus incremental economic profit). No further work needs to be done. However, if a relatively short horizon is used, for instance, 1 to 5 years, then simply compute the present value of the free cash flows (or economic profit) over the period. The explicit forecast period should be long enough to capture the current set of strategies that achieve attainable goals for the firm and long enough until the firm earns a constant, sustainable return on investment.

C. *Estimate the valuation parameters and calculate the continuing value as of the end of the explicit forecast period.* Valuation parameters include capital growth, *g,* return on incremental capital during the continuing value period, *r,* weighted average cost of capital, WACC, and NOPLAT.

D. *Discount the continuing value to the present.* Since the step 3 continuing value is itself a present value *as of the end of* the explicit forecast period, this amount needs to be valued back to the current date at the weighted-average cost of capital.

2. Using the template we have:

Assumptions		Years 1–3 (%)		Years 4+ (%)
ROIC		18		11
Growth		20		7
WACC		14		12

3-year horizon	1	2	3	CV base
NOPLAT	10.00	12.00	14.40	15.41
Depreciation	2.50	3.00	3.60	
Gross cash flow	12.50	15.00	18.00	
Gross investment	(13.61)	(16.33)	(19.60)	
Free cash flow	(1.11)	(1.33)	(1.60)	
Discount factor	0.8772	0.7695	0.6750	
Present value FCF	(0.97)	(1.03)	(1.08)	
PV FCF 1–3	(3.08)			
PV CV	75.64			
Total value	72.56			

5-year horizon	1	2	3	4	5	CV base
NOPLAT	10.00	12.00	14.40	15.41	16.49	17.64
Depreciation	2.50	3.00	3.60	3.85	4.12	
Gross cash flow	12.50	15.00	18.00	19.26	20.61	
Gross investment	(13.61)	(16.33)	(19.60)	(13.66)	(14.61)	
Free cash flow	(1.11)	(1.33)	(1.60)	5.60	6.00	
Discount factor	0.8772	0.7695	0.6750	0.6027	0.5381	
Present value FCF	(0.97)	(1.03)	(1.08)	3.38	3.23	
PV FCF 1–3	3.53					
PV CV	69.03					
Total value	72.56					

Value is the same for each horizon. This is only because the calculation for free cash and its present value is consistent over the two cases. For the 3-year horizon, and the first three years of the 5-year horizon, the calculations are identical. The first two years of the 3-year horizon CV base and years 4 and 5 of the 5-year horizon are also identical. This can be noticed by looking at the free cash flows for the explicit forecast period in the 5-year horizon. For years 1 to 3, the negative free cash flows dive from gross investment that exceeds gross cash flow. This in turn results from a growth rate that exceeds the ability of those assets to return a profit during those years. Years 4 and 5 yield free cash flows that are positive. In those years of the explicit forecast, growth is less than return on new investment, which returns a surplus cash flow, just as it does, by assumption, for the CV base year and thereon into the 75-plus years that effectively comprise the growing perpetuity. All that has happened in the valuation is a different split on the same value. For the short term forecast, the explicit forecast period produces (3.08) in present value with the rest of the 75.64 of continuing base value. The longer run horizon split is a positive 3.53 for the explicit forecast plus a commensurately lower CV base value of

69.03. Both add up to the same amount, 72.56 because both are effectively using the same cash flow streams.

Gross investment for any year is:

$$\text{NOPLAT}\left(\frac{1-g}{\text{ROIC}}\right)+\text{Depreciation}$$

The CV is the present value of the first year's CV base free cash flow, NOPLAT(1 − g/ROIC), discounted as a growing perpetuity:

$$\frac{\text{NOPLAT}\left(\dfrac{1-g}{\text{ROIC}}\right)}{(\text{WACC}-g)}$$

for years 4+.

3. Here's the algebra: Assume a 2-period explicit forecast horizon, weighted average cost of capital w, return on invested capital r, net operating profit after adjusted taxes N, invested capital C, capital growth rate g. We let date 0 be the beginning of the first period and the date at which valuation occurs; dates 1 and 2 are the ends of periods 1 and 2 respectively; date 3 is the end of the first period in the continuing base time frame. The value, V_0, of the entity is the present value of free cash flow:

$$V_0 = \frac{\left[N_1-\left(C_1-C_0\right)\right]}{(1+w)^1}+\frac{\left[N_2-\left(C_2-C_1\right)\right]}{(1+w)^2}+\frac{\left[\dfrac{N_3-\left(C_3-C_2\right)}{w-g}\right]}{(1+w)^2}$$

where the first two terms are the present value of NOPLAT less net investment, the change in invested capital from the end of the previous period to the end of the current period, and the third term is the present value of the growing free cash flow perpetuity.

To construct an equivalent economic profit version of the free cash flow valuation, add and subtract wC_0 in the numerator of the first term, and similarly add and subtract wC_1 in the numerator of the second term. This operation is algebraically neutral so that we still have the same free cash flow valuation as when we started. The resulting, and really not so tedious algebra, gives us:

$$V_0 = C_0 + \frac{\left(N_1 - w\,C_0\right)}{(1+w)^1} - \frac{C_1}{(1+w)^1}$$

$$+ \frac{C_1}{(1+w)^1} + \frac{\left(N_2 - w\,C_1\right)}{(1+w)^2} - \frac{C_2}{(1+w)^2}$$

$$+ \frac{\left[\dfrac{\left(N_3 - C_3 + C_2\right)}{(w-g)}\right]}{(1+w)^2}$$

Now take the $-C_2/(1+w)^2$ in the second line, multiply it by one, that is, by $(w-g)/(w-g)$, and incorporate it into the growing perpetuity term in the third line. In the mean time let terms in C_1 add up to zero in the first and second lines. After all of this we have:

$$V_0 = C_0 + \frac{\left(N_1 - w\,C_0\right)}{(1+w)^1} + \frac{\left(N_2 - w\,C_1\right)}{(1+w)^2} + \frac{\left[\dfrac{N_3 - C_3 + C_2}{(w-g)} - \dfrac{C_2(w-g)}{(w-g)}\right]}{(1+w)^2}$$

The third line is the present value of the continuing value base. We multiply C_2 through by $(w-g)$ and rearrange terms to get the equivalent term

$$\frac{\left\{\dfrac{\left(N_3 - wC_2\right)}{(w-g)} + \dfrac{\left[gC_2 - \left(C_3 - C_2\right)\right]}{(w-g)}\right\}}{(1+w)^2}$$

We realize that:

$$C_3 = C_2 + gC_2 \quad \text{or} \quad gC_2 = C_3 - C_2,$$

so that the numerator of the second term in the brackets equals zero. Finally, we have shown that the original free cash flow valuation V_0 is:

$$V_0 = C_0 + \frac{(N_1 - w\,C_0)}{(1+w)^1} + \frac{(N_2 - w\,C_1)}{(1+w)^2} + \frac{\left[\dfrac{(N_3 - w\,C_2)}{(w-g)}\right]}{(1+w)^2}$$

The value of the entity using free cash flows is the present value of the free cash flows in each explicit forecast period plus the present value of the growing free cash flow perpetuity in the continuing base period. The value of the entity using economic profit is the initial capital base plus the present value of economic profit for the explicit forecast period plus the present value of the growing economic profit perpetuity during the continuing base period.

4. A numerical example will illustrate this tedious algebra, and will also show that the valuation is robust to different assumptions about the weighted average cost of capital between the explicit forecast period and the continuing base period. Net investment t is: $(g_t/\text{ROIC}_t)\text{NOPLAT}_t$. NOPLAT_{t+1} is $\text{NOPLAT}_t\,(1 + g)$. Beginning capital plus net investment equals new capital:

Assumptions	Years 1–3 (%)			Years 4+ (%)
ROIC	18.00			15.75
Growth	20.00			5.00
WACC	14.00			12.00

3-year horizon	1	2	3	CV base
NOPLAT	10.00	12.00	14.40	15.12
Net investment	(11.11)	(13.33)	(16.00)	
Free cash flow	(1.11)	(1.33)	(1.60)	
Beginning IC	55.56	66.67	80.00	
Net investment	11.11	13.33	16.00	
New IC	66.67	80.00	96.00	
NOPLAT	10.00	12.00	14.40	
Capital charge	(7.78)	(9.33)	(11.20)	
Economic profit	2.22	2.67	3.20	
Discount factor	0.8772	0.7695	0.6750	
Present value FCF	(0.97)	(1.03)	(1.08)	
Present value EP	1.95	2.05	2.16	
PV FCF 1–3	(3.08)			
PV CV FCF	99.51			
Total value	96.43			
PV EP 1–3	6.16			
PV CV	34.71			
IC	55.56			
Total value	96.43			

In this example economic profit is positive while free cash flow is negative during the explicit forecast period. The firm is value adding while at the same time requiring net new investment in excess of operating earnings. A critical assumption for the operation of the model is that the ROIC (15.75%) for the continuing base period must be consistent with continuing base period

NOPLAT and the level of capital at the end of the explicit forecast period (equivalently the beginning of the continuing base
period).

The free cash flow model shows the firm how much fund-
ing is being generated or is needed during forecast periods. This
representation would certainly be useful to the corporate treas-
urer and the maintenance of long-run goals for the firm's money
desk and bank cash management relationships. The economic
profit valuation shows the firm how much value is gained or lost
during forecast periods. The primary audience for this representation would be banks and other contractual claimants on the
firm's ability to generate earnings.

If value based management is founded on value-adding activities, then the economic profit representation motivates the
judgment that negative free cash flows during the explicit forecast period are fine as long as they add value in the future. Already the future has been discounted by markets. The weighted
average cost of capital represents risk premia assessed by the
market regarding the ability of the entity to add forward value.
This representation is useful for value-based managers who are
required by agency relationships with stakeholders (specifically
shareholders) to add value or at least minimize the occurrence
of value-detracting activities. The economic profit profile of the
firm summarizes the short-term, within period, effects of long-
run, value-maximizing activities and strategies. The primary
audiences for the economic profit representation would be
shareholders and managers whose compensation is value based
and other managers who need to see how their achievement of
short-run targets affect long-run value added.

5. In this example, IMT is forecasted to have a 10 percent to 15
   percent to 20 percent sales growth over the explicit forecast period. NOPLAT for the continuing value base is forecasted from
   the desired 4 percent rate of growth for the firm into the long
   run. ROIC is then calculated at the CV NOPLAT as a percent of
   2002 invested capital. The investment rate of 35.15 percent
   then results in positive free cash flow.

IMT valuation	H 1999	F 2000	F 2001	F 2002	CV 2003
Working capital	193.000	212.231	244.066	292.879	—
Net fixed assets	246.000	271.656	312.404	374.885	—
Invested capital	439.000	483.887	556.470	667.764	694.475
Net investment		44.887	72.583	111.294	26.711
Debt	314.000	338.721	378.400	434.047	451.409
Equity	125.000	145.166	178.071	233.718	243.066
Sales growth		10.00%	15.00%	20.00%	
Net sales	1,029.000	1,131.900	1,301.685	1,562.022	
Operating expenses		(848.925)	(963.247)	(1,124.656)	
General expenses		(210.533)	(242.113)	(281.164)	
Depreciation		(28.600)	(32.890)	(39.468)	
Earnings before interest and tax		43.842	63.435	116.735	
Taxes on EBIT		(17.537)	(25.374)	(46.694)	
Change in deferred tax		2.196	2.525	3.030	
Net operating profit less adj tax		28.501	40.586	73.071	75.994
ROIC	13.48%	6.49%	8.39%	13.13%	11.38%
D/IC	71.53%	70.00%	68.00%	65.00%	65.00%
Eq/IC	28.47%	30.00%	32.00%	35.00%	35.00%
Tax rate	−21.62%	40.00%	40.00%	40.00%	40.00%
Interest rate	5.10%	6.00%	7.00%	7.00%	5.00%
Growth (investment/ capital)		10.22%	15.00%	20.00%	4.00%
Investment rate (Gwh/ROIC)		157.49%	178.84%	152.31%	35.15%
EBIT/sales		3.8733%	4.8733%	7.4733%	
Sales/IC		2.5784	2.6901	2.8070	
WC/sales	18.7561%	18.7500%	18.7500%	18.7500%	
NFAOA/sales	23.9067%	24.0000%	24.0000%	24.0000%	
Operating expenses/sales	74.3440%	75.0000%	74.0000%	72.0000%	74.0000%
SG&A/sales	18.5617%	18.6000%	18.6000%	18.0000%	18.6000%
Depreciation/sales	2.5267%	2.5267%	2.5267%	2.5267%	2.5267%
Change in deferred tax/sales	0.194%	0.194%	0.194%	0.194%	0.194%
Free cash flow		(16.386)	(31.997)	(38.223)	49.283
Cost of capital		7.82%	8.27%	8.33%	7.55%
Economic profit		(5.812)	0.558	26.738	25.603
Beta	1.73	1.942	1.821	1.665	1.665
Unlevered beta	0.4266	0.5827	0.5827	0.5827	0.5827
PV factors	1	0.927504	0.856641	0.790798	

IMT valuation	H 1999	F 2000	F 2001	F 2002	CV 2003
	PV Sums				
PV short term forecast	(72.835)	(15.198)	(27.410)	(30.227)	
Continuing value				1,389.751	
PV continuing value	1,099.012				
Value of IMT	1,026.177				
Debt	(314.000)				
Market value of equity	712.177				
Number of shares	33.7				
Stock price	21.13				
PV EP 1–3	16.232	(5.391)	0.478	21.145	
Continuing value				721.986	
PV CV	570.945				
IC	439.000				
Value of IMT	1,026.177				

With 33.7 million outstanding shares, IMT can rationalize a $21.13 share value using these numbers. Notice the path of free cash flow versus economic profit. Free cash flow is naturally negative during the expansion envisioned in the explicit forecast period from 2000 through 2003. At the same time economic profit starts negative but by 2001 becomes positive and lays the foundation for long run positive value addition in the continuing value base period.

13

Calculating and Interpreting the Results

---

1. There are two interrelated steps:

   A. *Calculate and test.* Discount the free cash flow, or economic profit, from explicit forecast and continuing value-base periods. Add investing capital to the economic profit value. Add in the value of non-operating net income and excess marketable securities, as well as the value of any nonrelated businesses. Subtract the value of debt and other nonequity forms of capital to get the market value of equity. Finally, divide the market value of equity by the number of average outstanding shares to derive a stock price. Perform this exercise for each scenario.

   B. *Interpret the results in the decision context.* For each scenario identify the operative assumptions, and their relationship to the various components of the valuation. The margin for error in each scenario can be adduced by changing key value drivers and noticing their effect on the entity value generated in a scenario. If the decision is to set a target debt to invested capital ratio, then a scenario with a 65 percent debt-to-capital ratio can be examined by changing capital growth, annual sales growth, operational ratios, and the like to see how sensitive value is to this decision. Be sure to examine alternative scenarios that might occur if interactive elements in the environment occur, such as competitive retaliation. The evaluation of additional scenarios might uncover further questions not already anticipated.

2. Here is the conservative, 3 percent forecast:

IMT valuation	H 1993	F 1994	F 1995	F 1996	CV 1997
WC	193.000	212.231	244.066	292.879	—
NFAOA	246.000	271.656	312.404	374.885	—
IC	439.000	483.887	556.470	667.764	681.120
Net investment		44.887	72.583	111.294	13.355
Debt	314.000	338.721	378.400	434.047	442.728
Equity	125.000	145.166	178.071	233.718	238.392
Sales growth		10.00%	15.00%	20.00%	
Net sales	1,029.000	1,131.900	1,301.685	1,562.022	
Operating expenses		(848.925)	(963.247)	(1,124.656)	
SG&A		(210.533)	(242.113)	(281.164)	
Depreciation		(28.600)	(32.890)	(39.468)	
Operating income		43.842	63.435	116.735	
Taxes on EBIT		(17.537)	(25.374)	(46.694)	
Change in deferred tax		2.196	2.525	3.030	
NOPLAT		28.501	40.586	73.071	74.532
ROIC	13.48%	6.49%	8.39%	13.13%	11.16%
D/IC	71.53%	70.00%	68.00%	65.00%	65.00%
Eq/IC	28.47%	30.00%	32.00%	35.00%	35.00%
Tax rate	−21.62%	40.00%	40.00%	40.00%	40.00%
Interest rate	5.10%	6.00%	7.00%	7.00%	5.00%
Growth (investment/capital)		10.22%	15.00%	20.00%	2.00%
Investment rate (Gwh/ROIC)		157.49%	178.84%	152.31%	17.92%
EBIT/sales		3.8733%	4.8733%	7.4733%	
Sales/IC		2.5784	2.6901	2.8070	
WC/sales	18.7561%	18.7500%	18.7500%	18.7500%	
NFAOA/sales	23.9067%	24.0000%	24.0000%	24.0000%	

IMT valuation	H 1993	F 1994	F 1995	F 1996	CV 1997
Operating expenses/sales	74.3440%	75.0000%	74.0000%	72.0000%	74.0000%
SG&A/sales	18.5617%	18.6000%	18.6000%	18.0000%	18.6000%
Depreciation/sales	2.5267%	2.5267%	2.5267%	2.5267%	2.5267%
Change in deferred tax/sales	0.194%	0.194%	0.194%	0.194%	0.194%
Free cash flow		(16.386)	(31.997)	(38.223)	61.177
Cost of capital		7.82%	8.27%	8.33%	7.55%
Economic profit		(5.812)	0.558	26.738	24.142
Beta	1.73	1.942	1.821	1.665	1.665
Unlevered beta	0.4266	0.5827	0.5827	0.5827	0.5827
PV factors	1	0.927504	0.856641	0.790798	
	PV Sums				
PV short term forecast	(72.835)	(15.198)	(27.410)	(30.227)	
Continuing value				1,103.047	
PV continuing value	872.288				
Value of IMT	799.453				
Debt	(314.000)				
Market value of equity	485.453				
Number of shares	33.7				
Stock price	14.41				
PV EP 1–3	16.232	(5.391)	0.478	21.145	
Continuing value				435.283	
PV CV	344.221				
IC	439.000				
Value of IMT	799.453				

The result is a $14.41 stock price. Large continuing value of economic profit promises long-run stability in IMT's value-creating activities. However, the stock is currently trading in the $18 to $24 range, so that this scenario and its resulting value indicates a loss of value position.

The medium performance scenario with 4 percent average industry growth indicates the following determination of value:

IMT valuation	H 1993	F 1994	F 1995	F 1996	CV 1997
WC	193.000	212.231	244.066	292.879	—
NFAOA	246.000	271.656	312.404	374.885	—
IC	439.000	483.887	556.470	667.764	694.475
Net investment		44.887	72.583	111.294	26.711
Debt	314.000	338.721	378.400	434.047	451.409
Equity	125.000	145.166	178.071	233.718	243.066
Sales growth		10.00%	15.00%	20.00%	
Net sales	1,029.000	1,131.900	1,301.685	1,562.022	
Operating expenses		(848.925)	(963.247)	(1,124.656)	
SG&A		(210.533)	(242.113)	(281.164)	
Depreciation		(28.600)	(32.890)	(39.468)	
Operating income		43.842	63.435	116.735	
Taxes on EBIT		(17.537)	(25.374)	(46.694)	
Change in deferred tax		2.196	2.525	3.030	
NOPLAT		28.501	40.586	73.071	75.994
ROIC	13.48%	6.49%	8.39%	13.13%	11.38%
D/IC	71.53%	70.00%	68.00%	65.00%	65.00%
Eq/IC	28.47%	30.00%	32.00%	35.00%	35.00%
Tax rate	−21.62%	40.00%	40.00%	40.00%	40.00%
Interest rate	5.10%	6.00%	7.00%	7.00%	5.00%
Growth (investment/capital)		10.22%	15.00%	20.00%	4.00%
Investment rate (Gwh/ROIC)		157.49%	178.84%	152.31%	35.15%
EBIT/sales		3.8733%	4.8733%	7.4733%	
Sales/IC		2.5784	2.6901	2.8070	
WC/sales	18.7561%	18.7500%	18.7500%	18.7500%	
NFAOA/sales	23.9067%	24.0000%	24.0000%	24.0000%	
Operating expenses/sales	74.3440%	75.0000%	74.0000%	72.0000%	74.0000%
SG&A/sales	18.5617%	18.6000%	18.6000%	18.0000%	18.6000%
Depreciation/sales	2.5267%	2.5267%	2.5267%	2.5267%	2.5267%
Change in deferred tax/sales	0.194%	0.194%	0.194%	0.194%	0.194%
Free cash flow		(16.386)	(31.997)	(38.223)	49.283
Cost of capital		7.82%	8.27%	8.33%	7.55%
Economic profit		(5.812)	0.558	26.738	25.603
Beta	1.73	1.942	1.821	1.665	1.665
Unlevered beta	0.4266	0.5827	0.5827	0.5827	0.5827
PV factors	1	0.927504	0.856641	0.790798	

IMT valuation	H 1993	F 1994	F 1995	F 1996	CV 1997
	PV Sums				
PV short term forecast	(72.835)	(15.198)	(27.410)	(30.227)	
Continuing value				1,389.751	
PV continuing value	1,099.012				
Value of IMT	1,026.177				
Debt	(314.000)				
Market value of equity	712.177				
Number of shares	33.7				
Stock price	21.13				
PV EP 1–3	16.232	(5.391)	0.478	21.145	
Continuing value				721.986	
PV CV	570.945				
IC	439.000				
Value of IMT	1,026.177				

In this scenario, at least the stock price begins to trade in the current range. This may be an indication of a validation of the model with the market's determination of current stock price.

An aggressive scenario would have IMT operate at the 6 percent long run growth level. On pages 190–191 is the probable, but unlikely outcome.

This scenario posts a stock price well above the current trading range. Even though a $45.27 stock price is highly unlikely, it possibly takes account of IMT resilience in its markets, including a lead on the development of CAD/CAM systems, and the extension of its machine tool development into new industries left as residual business by its key Japanese and German *mittelstand* competitors.

If we assign a probability of 30 percent to the conservative scenario, 60 percent to the medium performance scenario, and

IMT valuation	H 1993	F 1994	F 195	F 1996	CV 1997
WC	193.000	212.231	244.066	292.879	—
NFAOA	246.000	271.656	312.404	374.885	—
IC	439.000	483.887	556.470	667.764	707.830
Net investment		44.887	72.583	111.294	40.066
Debt	314.000	338.721	378.400	434.047	460.090
Equity	125.000	145.166	178.071	233.718	247.741
Sales growth		10.00%	15.00%	20.00%	
Net sales	1,029.000	1,131.900	1,301.685	1,562.022	
Operating expenses		(848.925)	(963.247)	(1,124.656)	
SG&A		(210.533)	(242.113)	(281.164)	
Depreciation		(28.600)	(32.890)	(39.468)	
Operating income		43.842	63.435	116.735	
Taxes on EBIT		(17.537)	(25.374)	(46.694)	
Change in deferred tax		2.196	2.525	3.030	
NOPLAT		28.501	40.586	73.071	77.455
ROIC	13.48%	6.49%	8.39%	13.13%	11.60%
D/IC	71.53%	70.00%	68.00%	65.00%	65.00%
Eq/IC	28.47%	30.00%	32.00%	35.00%	35.00%
Tax rate	−21.62%	40.00%	40.00%	40.00%	40.00%
Interest rate	5.10%	6.00%	7.00%	7.00%	5.00%
Growth (investment/capital)		10.22%	15.00%	20.00%	6.00%
Investment rate (Gwh/ROIC)		157.49%	178.84%	152.31%	51.73%
EBIT/sales		3.8733%	4.8733%	7.4733%	
Sales/IC		2.5784	2.6901	2.8070	
WC/sales	18.7561%	18.7500%	18.7500%	18.7500%	
NFAOA/sales	23.9067%	24.0000%	24.0000%	24.0000%	
Operating expenses/sales	74.3440%	75.0000%	74.0000%	72.0000%	74.0000%
SG&A/sales	18.5617%	18.6000%	18.6000%	18.0000%	18.6000%
Depreciation/sales	2.5267%	2.5267%	2.5267%	2.5267%	2.5267%
Change in deferred tax/sales	0.194%	0.194%	0.194%	0.194%	0.194%
Free cash flow		(16.386)	(31.997)	(38.223)	37.389
Cost of capital		7.82%	8.27%	8.33%	7.55%
Economic profit		(5.812)	0.558	26.738	27.065
Beta	1.73	1.942	1.821	1.665	1.665
Unlevered beta	0.4266	0.5827	0.5827	0.5827	0.5827
PV factors	1	0.927504	0.856641	0.790798	

IMT valuation	H 1999	F 2000	F 2001	F 2002	CV 2003
	PV Sums				
PV short term forecast	(72.835)	(15.198)	(27.410)	(30.227)	
Continuing value				2,418.153	
PV continuing value	1,912.270				
Value of IMT	1,839.435				
Debt	(314.000)				
Market value of equity	1,525.435				
Number of shares	33.7				
Stock price	45.27				
PV EP 1–3	16.232	(5.391)	0.478	21.145	
Continuing value				1,750.388	
PV CV	1,384.203				
IC	439.000				
Value of IMT	1,839.435				

10 percent to the aggressive scenario, then the models forecast a stock price of:

$$(0.3)(14.41) + (0.6)(21.13) + (0.1)(45.27) = 21.52$$

right where the market thinks it should be trading. This would be a hold recommendation for investors who believe the drivers and construction of this model.

3. There are at least four common pitfalls: modeling short cuts, hockey stick forecasts, short forecast horizons, and double counting of undervalued or fully depreciated assets.

   A. *Short cuts are used in this model.* For example, aggregated balance sheet items, such as "net fixed and other assets" might have sufficient variation in them to cause differential opinions as to the value of the invested capital forecasts. The analysis of key drivers, such as operating ratios, ought to be based on a five to ten year historical analysis. That analysis was performed in previous exercises. What was not yet produced is a similar historical analysis of key players in the industry.

B. *Sales growth "hockey sticks."* The usual pitfall of employing earnings or sales "hockey sticks" was avoided in this analysis. Sales growth averaged about 60 percent per year over the last five years: clearly a hockey stick based on historical fact. Cooler heads prevailed in the analysis of future sales growth estimated in this model.

C. *Short forecast horizons.* The use of three years will encourage strategic thinking only over a three-year horizon. Longer horizons of 5- to 7-years are better in that they force planners and line managers to be explicit about the longer run consequences of their short run actions.

D. *Double counting of undervalued assets.* This is a final pitfall. Examples of such assets would be plant and equipment long depreciated on the books, but still producing earnings value. These should have been already included *de facto* in the production of sales through expenses.

14

Multibusiness Valuation

1. The cost of capital *rises* when business risk *rises,* tax rates *fall,*
   new investment *increases,* and new debt *decreases.* Why? A
   very long explanation follows (with a little algebra for a chaser):

   If a firm expected to earn NOPLAT in perpetuity and the return is k, under all equity financing, the value of this unlevered firm is:

   $$V_U = \frac{\text{NOPLAT}}{r} = \frac{\text{NOI}(1-T)}{k}$$

   Where NOPLAT = Net operating income (NOI) after taxes
   T = Marginal corporate tax rate

   Suppose a similar firm, with the same operating or business
   risk, has a face value of perpetual debt, D, paying out r_d rate
   of interest. Net income to shareholders, *NI,* is:

   $$\text{NI} = (\text{NOI} - r_d D)(1-T) = \text{NOI}(1-T) - r_d D + r_d DT$$

   Add $r_d D$ to both sides to get the total payment available to
   bond and shareholders and thus to the operation as a whole:

   $$\text{NI} + r_d D = \text{NOI}(1-T) + r_d DT$$

Thus, total operational cash flow is the after-tax net operating income (like the unlevered firm), plus the debt tax shield. The riskiness of the after-tax NOI for the levered firm is the same as the riskiness of the unlevered firm, thus both should earn r. The riskiness of the debt tax shield is impounded in the perpetual yield, k_d. The market value of the debt (B for market value; D for face value) is:

$$B = \frac{r_d D}{k_d}$$

The present value of the levered firm becomes:

$$V_L = \frac{\text{NOI}(1-T)}{k} + TB = V_U + TB$$

The gain from leverage is the extra value that the interest tax shield provides to the otherwise unlevered firm value.

The weighted average cost of capital is determined from the relationship between the levered and unlevered firm value:

$$V_L = \frac{r_d D}{k_d} + \frac{\text{NI}}{k_e} = B + S = \frac{\text{NOI}(1-T)}{k} + TB$$

If we examine the effect of new investment, ΔA, on the value of the levered firm we can calculate the cost of acquiring another dollar of capital:

$$\frac{\Delta V_L}{\Delta A} = \frac{\Delta \text{NOI}(1-T)}{\Delta Ak} + \frac{T\Delta B}{\Delta A} = \frac{\Delta S_{old}}{\Delta A} + \frac{\Delta S_{new}}{\Delta A} + \frac{\Delta B}{\Delta A}$$

$$= \frac{\Delta S_{old}}{\Delta A} + \frac{(\Delta S_{new} + \Delta B)}{\Delta A}$$

and since new assets are acquired by issuing new debt and stock, $\Delta A = \Delta S_{new} + \Delta B$, so that

$$\frac{\Delta V_L}{\Delta A} = \frac{\Delta \text{NOI}(1-T)}{\Delta Ak} + \frac{T\Delta B}{\Delta A} = \frac{\Delta S_{old}}{\Delta A} + 1$$

The criterion for taking on more assets is that the old share-holders will be better off materially. New investment demands that the change in old shareholder value increase with increase in the asset base:

$$\frac{\Delta S_{old}}{\Delta A} > 0$$

This can happen only if:

$$\frac{\Delta S_{old}}{\Delta A} > 0 \quad \text{or} \quad \frac{\Delta S_{old}}{\Delta A} + 1 > 1$$

That is if:

$$\frac{\Delta NOI(1-T)}{\Delta A} > k\left(\frac{1-T\,\Delta B}{\Delta A}\right)$$

The term on the left-hand side is the marginal return on invested capital. The term on the right-hand side is the cost of invested capital expressed in terms of leverage and business risk. This result harks back to the discussion of economic profit. Grow the firm, that is, $\Delta A > 0$, only if the return on invested capital exceeds the cost of capital. Shareholders will be profitable only if new investment creates economic profit. This is the derivation of the economic profit criterion.

2. The cost of equity *increases* with business risk and *leverage*. *Higher* bond rates and tax rates *lower* the cost of equity. Another algebraic explanation follows:

Let's assume a world with corporate taxes at the marginal rate of T, corporate debt with expected cost per unit of principal, r_d; yield of k_d; market value, B; equity with expected cost, k_e; and market value, S. The weighted average cost of capital is then:

$$r_a = \frac{r_d(1-\tau)B}{A} + \frac{r_e S}{A}$$

where $A = B + S$ is the market value of long-run operating assets. If r_a represents the required rate of return on operating assets, this rate of return represents the compensation required by investors for undertaking the business risk of the whole firm, no matter how it happens to be financed. If this is the return, whatever the financing, the firm might as well be 100 percent equity financed for this rate of return. Call the return on 100 percent equity financing that represents the firm's operating asset risk, the "unlevered" return, and denote this return by r_u. With this kind of thinking, $r_a = r_u$. Multiply both sides of the WACC equation by A/E then solve for r_e to get:

$$k_e = \frac{k_a A}{S} - \frac{k_d(1-\tau)B}{S}$$

Realize that $A = B + S$ and simplify the expression to get:

$$k_e = k_a + \frac{\left[k_a - k_d(1-\tau)\right]B}{S}$$

Now substitute the cost of capital expression from the previous question into this equation, that is, let:

$$k_a = k\left(1 - T\frac{\Delta B}{\Delta A}\right) = k\left(1 - T\frac{B}{A}\right)$$

where the Δ's are shown from the equation in an attempt to use a target debt-to-equity ratio that replaces a marginal ratio. This procedure is valid if every new dollar of capital requires the issuing of a prescribed amount of new debt, with the rest of the capital raised by issuing new stock. Making the substitution, we have the following expression for the cost of equity:

$$k_e = k\left(1 - T\frac{B}{A}\right) + \frac{\left[k\left(1 - T\frac{B}{A}\right) - k_d(1-\tau)\right]B}{S}$$

$$= k + \frac{(1-T)(k - k_d)B}{S}$$

The cost of equity increases with business risk and leverage. Higher bond rates and tax rates lower the cost of equity.

3. In a world without taxes, the beta on an equivalent firm without debt, unlevered beta or β_u, is found from the relationship:

$$\beta_L = \beta_u \left[1 + (1-T)\frac{D}{E} \right]$$

Where D/E = The target long term debt (plus debt in current liabilities) to equity (including equity equivalents such as deferred taxes) ratio. The beta of a firm with business risk similar to your company, but without debt is:

$$\beta_u = \frac{\beta_L}{\left[1+(1-T)\dfrac{D}{E} \right]} = \frac{1.009}{\left[1+(1-.4)\dfrac{1}{3} \right]} = 0.840833$$

Where T = The marginal corporate tax rate. If a 10-year treasury bond yield is 7 percent (from stripped treasuries quotes) and the market risk premium is 6 percent, then the unlevered equivalent return is:

$$k_u = 7 + 0.840833(6) = 13.054\%$$

As your company expands its operations and takes on more debt, it changes its debt-to-equity ratio. If the company does not at the same time increase or decrease its business risk, then we can use the following formula to calculate the new equity beta associated with each new D/E scenario:

$$\beta_L = 0.840833 \left[1 + .6\frac{D}{E} \right]$$

We then substitute the value of β_L into the equity returns model to determine the new cost of equity capital at different debt-to-equity ratios. The following table summarizes the relationship:

Debt equity	0.33	0.67	1.00	1.50	3.00
Unlevered beta	0.840833	0.840833	0.840833	0.840833	0.840833
Tax rate	40%	40%	40%	40%	40%
Levered beta	1.009	1.177	1.345	1.598	2.354
Unlevered return	12.045%	12.045%	12.045%	12.045%	12.045%
Levered return	13.054%	14.063%	15.072%	16.585%	21.126%
Financial risk	1.009%	2.018%	3.027%	4.540%	9.081%

Increasing the amount of debt has the effect of increasing the amount of financial risk to the shareholders.

4. The calculations proceed in the following steps:

  A. The total industry debt (book value), market value of equity (price times shares outstanding) and invested capital (debt plus market value of equity) is computed. This will be used to weight the unlevered beta's from each firm in the analysis.

  B. Each firm's debt-to-invested capital and market equity-to-invested capital is calculated.

  C. Unlevered beta is then computed as $\beta_u = \beta_L/[1 + (1 - T) D/E]$, where the D/E ratio is the ratio of the debt and equity to asset ratios, and a 34 percent tax rate is assumed. Average industry unlevered beta is the invested capital weighted average of the series of firms' unlevered beta's.

  D. The average industry unlevered beta is relevered using the project's expected D/E ratio: $0.20/(1 - 0.20) = 1/4$. The project equity required rate-of-return is computed using a 10-year treasury note rate of 8 percent and a market risk premium of 5.5 percent.

Industry debt	$ 8,452,000			
Industry market equity	42,374,525			
Industry invested capital	50,826,525			

	Dow	Dupont	Olin	United
Market equity	$15,554,450	$20,116,600	$1,025,000	$5,678,475
Invested capital	$18,892,450	$23,348,600	$1,499,000	$7,086,475
LTD/IC	17.67%	13.84%	31.62%	19.87%
MVE/IC	82.33%	86.16%	68.38%	80.13%
Unlevered beta	1.0949	1.0397	0.9960	1.0742
IC/Industry IC	37.17%	45.94%	2.95%	13.94%
Industry unlevered beta	1.0638			
Project leverage	20.00%			
Project equity beta	1.2393			
Project equity required return	15.32%			

15

Valuing Dot.coms

1.

Issue	Resolution
A. They don't make any money the first few years.	Don't use PE, revenue multiples; they are backward looking.
	Use economic fundamentals.
B. The companies exhibit hyper-growth rates.	Start with fixed point in future and work backward to the present using economic fundamentals to parse sources of growth.
C. The fate of these companies is highly uncertain.	Develop probability weighted scenarios explicitly.

2.

   A.

Value driver	Relation to growth
Penetration rate	Ability to enter new markets and acquire share of market to drive revenue growth.
Average revenue per customer	Exposes range of customer diversification and segment profitability and drives.
Sustainable growth margin	Platform for future growth, insured returns on invested capital composed of cost of customer acquisition and customer contribution margin; also relates to amount of capital needed to support revenue.
Capital	Amount of sales supported by capital is influenced by "clicks" versus "bricks" and mortar and working capital; also the market perception of riskiness of cash flow.
Date when growth begins	Earlier preempts competitive movement; later allows substitutes and new service entrants.

B.

Driver	Low scenario	Medium scenario	High scenario
Total market size	1 billion	1 billion	1 billion
Market share	10%	12%	15%
Average revenue per customer	$300	$500	$600
Contribution margin per customer	10%	14%	18%
Average cost of acquisition per customer	$75	$50	$50
Proportion of customers lost each year	30%	25%	20%
Sales per capital	2.0	2.5	3.4
Growth	5%	12%	14%
Probability	30%	60%	10%
Date when growth begins	2010	2010	2010

C. Calculated discounted cash flow value. Assuming a 25 percent cost of capital.

Item	Calculation	Low scenario
Revenue	Total number × Share × Revenue per customer	$40,000,000,000
Contribution margin	Total number × Share × Contribution per customer	4,000,000,000
Acquisition cost	Total number × Share × Acquisition cost × Churn rate	1,875,000,000
EBIT	Contribution margin − Acquisition cost	2,125,000,000
Tax	Tax rate × EBIT	850,000,000
Net operating profit less tax	EBIT − Tax	1,275,000,000
Invested capital	Revenue/Sales turns	$20,000,000,000
ROIC	NOPLAT/ Invested capital	6%
Growth	Assumption	5%
Reinvestment rate	Growth/ROIC	78.431%
Free cash flow	NOPLAT × (1 − Reinvestment rate)	275,000,000
Cost of capital	Assumption	25%
Continuing value	Free cash flow/ (Cost of capital − Growth)	1,375,000,000
Discounted cash flow	Continuing value/ (1 + Cost of capital) 10	147,639,501
Number of customers	Total number × Share	100,000,000
Value per customer	Discounted cash flow/Number of customers	1.48

D.

Item	Low scenario	Medium scenario	High scenario
Revenue	$40,000,000,000	$60,000,000,000	$77,000,000,000
Contribution margin	4,000,000,000	8,400,000,000	13,860,000,000
Acquisition cost	1,875,000,000	1,500,000,000	1,750,000,000
EBIT	2,125,000,000	6,900,000,000	12,110,000,000
Tax	850,000,000	2,760,000,000	4,844,000,000
Net operating profit less tax	1,275,000,000	4,140,000,000	7,266,000,000
Invested capital	20,000,000,000	24,000,000,000	22,647,058,824
ROIC	6%	17%	32%
Growth	5%	12%	14%
Reinvestment rate	78.431%	69.565%	43.636%
Free cash flow	275,000,000	1,260,000,000	4,095,411,765
Cost of capital	25%	25%	25%
Continuing value	1,375,000,000	9,692,307,692	37,231,016,043
Discounted cash flow	147,639,501	1,040,703,614	3,997,649,908
Number of customers	100,000,000	120,000,000	140,000,000
Value per customer	1.48	8.67	28.55
Expected value	$ 1,068,479,009		

16

Valuing Cyclical Companies

1. Two reasons are:
   A. Base years will either be too high or too low as a basis for forecasting future cash flows.
   B. Share prices reflect high levels of volatility.

2. The steps are:
   A. Use past cycles to value the normal-cycle scenario.
   B. Use recent performance to construct a new-trend-line scenario.
   C. Consider supply and demand growth, new entries and exits from the industry, technology, and government changes as the rationale for the two scenarios.
   D. Assign probabilities to each scenario and calculate expected value.

3. Two scenarios are produced: a normal scenario that will be defined (naively!) as the average scenario over the last five years and a new-trend scenario that will reflect both industry and GP recent activity.
   A. The normal scenario is produced from the following data:

	1995	1996	1997	1998	1999
Invested capital statement					
Working capital	831	125	(104)	(3)	368
Long term assets	9,740	10,203	10,034	10,055	12,338
Operating invested capital	10,571	10,328	9,930	10,052	12,706
Net investment		(243)	(398)	122	2,654
Debt	7,052	6,817	6,460	6,928	8,831
Equity	3,519	3,511	3,470	3,124	3,875
					22.50
NOPLAT statement					
Sales	14,313	13,024	13,094	13,342	17,977
Operating expenses	(9,794)	(9,798)	(10,209)	(10,231)	(13,333)
General expenses	(1,406)	(1,475)	(1,296)	(1,204)	(1,670)
Depreciation	(984)	(996)	(1,017)	(997)	(1,013)
EBIT	2,129	755	572	910	1,961
Taxes on EBIT	(852)	(350)	(346)	(386)	(759)
Change in deferred taxes	10	14	100	38	73
NOPLAT	1,287	419	326	562	1,275
Provision for income taxes	679	135	106	202	705
Tax shield on interest expense	173	213	282	188	192
Tax on investment income	—	—	(78)	(10)	(137)
Tax on non-operating income	—	2	36	6	—
Taxes on EBIT	852	350	346	386	759
Net income statement					
Sales	14,313	13,024	13,094	13,342	17,977
Operating expenses	(9,794)	(9,798)	(10,209)	(10,231)	(13,333)
General expenses	(1,406)	(1,475)	(1,296)	(1,204)	(1,670)
Depreciation	(984)	(996)	(1,017)	(997)	(1,013)
EBIT	2,129	755	572	910	1,961
Investment income	—	—	128	24	355
Investment expense	(432)	(459)	(465)	(443)	(495)
Miscellaneous, net	—	(5)	(60)	(15)	—
Earnings before taxes	1,697	291	175	476	1,821
Income taxes	(679)	(135)	(106)	(202)	(705)
Net income (before extra items)	1,018	156	69	274	1,116
Tax rate	−40%	−46%	−61%	−42%	−39%

	1995	1996	1997	1998	1999
Reconciliation to net income statement					
Net income	1,018	156	69	274	1,116
Add: increase in deferred taxes	10	14	100	38	73
Adjusted net income	1,028	170	169	312	1,189
Add: Interest expense after tax	259	246	183	255	303
Income available to investors	1,287	416	352	567	1,492
Less: Interest income after tax	—	—	(50)	(14)	(218)
Less: Non-operating income after tax	—	3	24	9	—
NOPLAT	1,287	419	326	562	1,275
ROIC tree					
ROIC		4.0%	3.2%	5.7%	12.7%
= (1 − EBIT cash tax rate)		55.5%	56.9%	61.7%	65.0%
× Pretax ROIC		7.1%	5.5%	9.2%	19.5%
= EBIT/Sales		5.8%	4.4%	6.8%	10.9%
× Sales/Invested capital		1.23	1.27	1.34	1.79
EBIT/Sales = 1 − (Operating expenses/Sales		75.2%	78.0%	76.7%	74.2%
+ General expenses/Sales		11.3%	9.9%	9.0%	9.3%
+ Depreciation/Sales)		7.6%	7.8%	7.5%	5.6%
Sales/Invested capital = 1 /(Operating working capital/Sales		6.4%	1.0%	−0.8%	0.0%
+ Long term operating assets/Sales)		74.8%	77.9%	75.2%	55.9%
Change in deferred tax/Sales		0.107%	0.764%	0.285%	0.406%
Free cash flow statement					
NOPLAT		419	326	562	1,275
Depreciation		996	1,017	997	1,013
Gross cash flow		1,415	1,343	1,559	2,288

	1995	1996	1997	1998	1999
Increase in operating working capital		(706)	(229)	101	371
Capital expenditures		1,459	848	1,018	3,296
Gross investment		753	619	1,119	3,667
Free cash flow		662	724	440	(1,379)
Non-operating cash flow		(5)	68	9	355
Cash flow available to investors		657	792	449	(1,024)
Cost of capital					
Beta		1.33	1.33	1.33	1.33
Debt/invested capital		66.7%	66.0%	65.1%	68.9%
Equity/invested capital		33.3%	34.0%	34.9%	31.1%
Cost of debt		6.5%	6.8%	6.9%	7.1%
Cost of equity		15.0%	15.0%	15.0%	15.0%
Weighted average cost of capital		7.3%	6.9%	7.8%	7.7%
Economic profit					
NOPLAT		418.7	325.5	561.8	1,274.8
Capital charge		(772.8)	(708.9)	(774.4)	(771.0)
Economic profit		(354.0)	(383.3)	(212.6)	503.8

Following the assumptions of average starting asset and sales, as well as average ratios and zero growth. One possible normal scenario produces this valuation:

	Average 1995–1999	F 2000	F 2001	F 2002	CV 2003
Working capital	243,400	254,752	266,634	279,070	—
Net fixed assets	10,474,000	10,962,507	11,473,798	12,008,935	—
Invested capital	10,717,400	11,217,259	11,740,431	12,288,005	12,861,117
Net investment		499,859	523,172	547,573	573,112
Debt	7,217,600	7,554,229	7,906,557	8,275,319	8,661,279
Equity	3,499,800	3,663,031	3,833,874	4,012,686	4,199,837
Sales growth		4.66%	4.66%	4.66%	
Net sales	14,350,000	15,019,283	15,719,782	16,452,952	
Operating expense		(11,170,788)	(11,691,793)	(12,237,098)	
General expense		(1,475,972)	(1,544,811)	(1,616,861)	
Depreciation		(1,048,105)	(1,096,989)	(1,148,152)	
EBIT		1,324,418	1,386,189	1,450,841	
Taxes on EBIT		(512,748)	(536,663)	(561,693)	
Change in deferred tax		58,654	61,389	64,253	
Net operating profit less adjusted tax		870,324	910,915	953,400	997,867
Net investment		(499,859)	(523,172)	(547,573)	(573,112)
Free cash flow		370,465	387,743	405,827	424,755
Cost of capital		7.46%	7.46%	7.46%	7.46%
Economic profit		70,822	74,125	77,582	81,201
Beta	1.37	1.368	1.368	1.368	1.368
Unlevered beta	0.6043	0.5827	0.5827	0.5827	0.5827
PV factors	1	0.930580162	0.865979439	0.805863287	

	Average 1995–1999	F 2000	F 2001	F 2002	CV 2003
	PV sums				
PV short term forecast	1,007,566	344,747	335,777	327,041	
Continuing value				15,192,342	
PV continuing value	12,242,951				
Market value of asset	13,250,516				
Debt	(7,217,600)				
Market value of equity	6,032,916				
Number of shares	172.3				
Stock price	35.01				
	Sum				
PV economic profit 1–3	192,617	65,906	64,191	62,521	
Continuing value				2,904,337	
PV continuing value	2,340,499				
Invested capital	10,717,400				
Market value of asset	13,250,516				
ROIC	6.36%	8.12%	8.12%	8.12%	8.12%
D/IC	67.34%	67.34%	67.34%	67.34%	67.34%
Eq/IC	32.66%	32.66%	32.66%	32.66%	32.66%
Tax rate	38.71%	38.71%	38.71%	38.71%	38.71%
Interest rate	6.83%	6.83%	6.83%	6.83%	6.83%
Growth (investment/ capital)		4.66%	4.66%	4.66%	4.66%
Investment rate (Gwh/ROIC)		57.43%	57.43%	57.43%	57.43%
EBIT/sales		8.8181%	8.8181%	8.8181%	
Sales/IC		1.4014	1.4014	1.4014	
WC/sales	1.6962%	1.6962%	1.6962%	1.6962%	
NFAOA/sales	72.9895%	72.9895%	72.9895%	72.9895%	
Operating expenses/sales	74.3763%	74.3763%	74.3763%	74.3763%	74.3763%
SG&A/sales	9.8272%	9.8272%	9.8272%	9.8272%	9.8272%
Deprecation/sales	6.9784%	6.9784%	6.9784%	6.9784%	6.9784%
Change in deferred tax/sales	0.391%	0.391%	0.391%	0.391%	0.391%

The normal scenario produces a stock price of $35.10 within the 5-year range of about $23 to $54 GP experienced between 1995 and 2000. A key driver of this average scenario is that ROIC exceeds the cost of capital in each forecast year and in perpetuity.

B. A new trend can be established from industry growth trends. For example, based on recent industry growth and GP's recent plans to attain and exceed industry efficiency, profitability, and growth standards, the following new-trend scenario assumptions can be made:

To attain 10.20 percent EBIT/sales, operating expenses must be no more than 73 percent of sales.

A financial engineering overhaul of debt-equity and pumped up investor relations may have little or no effect on beta in the cyclical paper and pulp industry, and thus, keep current beta levels at about 1.37. This also encourages managers to achieve higher shareholder return expectations and take more risks controlled by realized results.

Maintain long run 4.66 percent sales growth. Increase near term sales growth to 8 percent.

Together these assumptions will produce the pro forma valuation shown on pages 212–213.

	Average 1995–1999	F 2000	F 2001	F 2002	CV 2003
Working capital	243,400	258,004	273,484	289,893	—
Net fixed assets	10,474,000	11,102,440	11,768,586	12,474,702	—
Invested capital	10,717,400	11,360,444	12,042,071	12,764,595	13,359,935
Net investment		643,044	681,627	722,524	595,340
Debt	7,217,600	7,650,656	8,109,695	8,596,277	8,997,207
Equity	3,499,800	3,709,788	3,932,375	4,168,318	4,362,728
Sales growth		6.00%	6.00%	6.00%	
Net sales	14,350,000	15,211,000	16,123,660	17,091,080	
Operating expense		(11,104,030)	(11,770,272)	(12,476,488)	
General expense		(1,494,812)	(1,584,501)	(1,679,571)	
Depreciation		(1,061,484)	(1,125,173)	(1,192,683)	
EBIT		1,550,674	1,643,714	1,742,337	
Taxes on EBIT		(600,343)	(636,364)	(674,546)	
Change in deferred tax		59,402	62,967	66,745	
Net operating profit less adjusted tax		1,009,733	1,070,317	1,134,536	1,187,451
Net investment		(643,044)	(681,627)	(722,524)	(595,340)
Free cash flow		366,689	388,690	412,012	592,111
Cost of capital		7.46%	7.46%	7.46%	7.46%
Economic profit		210,232	222,846	236,216	235,232
Beta	1.37	1.368	1.368	1.368	1.368
Unlevered beta	0.6043	0.5827	0.5827	0.5827	0.5827
PV factors	1	0.930580162	0.865979439	0.805863287	
	PV sums				
PV short term forecast	1,009,857	341,234	336,598	332,025	
Continuing value				21,178,205	
PV continuing value	17,066,738				
Market value of asset	18,076,594				
Debt	(7,217,600)				
Market value of equity	10,858,994				
Number of shares	172.3				
Stock price	63.02				

	Average 1995–1999	F 2000	F 2001	F 2002	CV 2003
	Sum				
PV economic profit 1–3	578,975	195,637	192,980	190,358	
Continuing value				8,413,610	
PV continuing value	6,780,219				
Invested capital	10,717,400				
Market value of asset	18,076,594				
ROIC	6.36%	9.42%	9.42%	9.42%	9.30%
D/IC	67.34%	67.34%	67.34%	67.34%	67.34%
Eq/IC	32.66%	32.66%	32.66%	32.66%	32.66%
Tax rate	38.71%	38.71%	38.71%	38.71%	38.71%
Interest rate	6.83%	6.83%	6.83%	6.83%	6.83%
Growth (Investment/ Capital)		6.00%	6.00%	6.00%	4.66%
Investment rate (Growth/ROIC)		63.68%	63.68%	63.68%	50.14%
EBIT/Sales		10.1944%	10.1944%	10.1944%	
Sales/IC		1.4193	1.4193	1.4193	
WC/Sales	1.6962%	1.6962%	1.6962%	1.6962%	
NFAOA/Sales	72.9895%	72.9895%	72.9895%	72.9895%	
Operating expenses/Sales	74.3763%	73.0000%	73.0000%	73.0000%	73.0000%
SG&A/Sales	9.8272%	9.8272%	9.8272%	9.8272%	9.8272%
Deprecation/Sales	6.9784%	6.9784%	6.9784%	6.9784%	6.9784%
Change in deferred tax/Sales	0.391%	0.391%	0.391%	0.391%	0.391%

These assumptions will result in a $63.02 share price, not quite double the normal scenario value.

C. Also, the analysis described in Chapter 6, "Making Value Happen," can be performed to justify each of the scenarios.

D. If the normal scenario occurs 70 percent of the time (based on IBES earnings forecast variations) and the new trend scenario occurs 30 percent of the time, then the stock price is about $45 per share.

Scenario	Probability (percent)	Value
Normal	70	35
New trend	30	63

17

Valuing Foreign Subsidiaries

1. There are four steps in the valuation process. They build on the valuation steps for a domestic firm with the extra consideration of foreign currency translation, the differences in accounting and regulatory environments, political risk, and the lack of comparably good and available data.

   A. *Calculate nominal cash flow in subsidiary's currency.* Account for hidden assets, foreign exchange translation. Use appropriate transfer prices, effective tax rates, and foreign inflation predictions.

   B. *Convert forward cash flows to subsidiary's currency using forward rates if not already in local currency.*

   C. *Estimate subsidiary's cost of capital.* Use the weighted average cost of capital estimation process to discount cash flows.

   D. *Estimate the subsidiary value in the parent's currency using the spot foreign exchange rate.*

2. Applying the methodology to Quebecor:

   A. *Calculate free cash flows in foreign currencies.* For Quebecor, this step involves the calculation of cash flows in Indian, U.S. dollar, French franc, and Mexican peso currencies.

The problem is complicated by the fact that the French printing subsidiary receives payments and makes disbursements in British pounds, Dutch guilders, and so on. Similar foreign currency cash flows exist in the other subsidiaries. To complicate issues further, accounting and depreciation differences in the various tax jurisdictions, inventory valuation, representations of fixed versus current assets and liabilities, all need to be addressed. Transfer pricing determines where profits will be reported and thus is a critical tax minimization activity.

B. *Use forward foreign exchange rates to convert cash flows into subsidiary's currency.* For the Imprimeries Fecome-Quebecor subsidiary, forward rates in guilders, marks, pounds, Swiss francs, lira, and so on, would have to be used to convert cash flows into French francs. Most of the U.S., Mexican, and Indian cash flows are already stated in local currencies. Interest rate parity is used to determine the relationship between spot and covered forward rates. The French subsidiary would need to forecast the forward relationship between British pounds and French francs during, a five-year explicit forecast period, as well as the long run relationships in the continuing base forecast. Separate components of cash flow can be handled this way.

C. *Estimate the subsidiary's cost of capital.* In this step, the main focus is to avoid using the Canadian parent's weighted average cost of capital to discount French, U.S., Mexican, and Indian cash flows. Also inappropriate is the ad hoc fudging of risk premia due to political considerations, such as the rise or fall of the new Mexican government or the economic success of the bail out of the peso. This is better handled by forecasting cash flows that are associated with appropriately constructed political risk scenarios, computing the expected value of cash flows, and discounting expected cash flow by the risk-adjusted expected required rate-of-return.

D. *Discount the subsidiary's free cash flow in local currency and convert to the parent's current at the spot rate.* Barring limitations to expatriating free cash flows to the parent

company, this step is straightforward. The French subsidiary's franc cash flows are discounted at the French risk-
adjusted rate. The French franc present value is then
converted to the parent by the application of the Canadian
dollar-to-French franc spot rate.

3. There are two methods available under FASB No. 8 and 52: current and temporal.

   A. *The current method* uses the recent exchange rate for all balance sheet items, except equity, and the average exchange
   rate for the reporting period for the income statement.

   B. *The temporal method* uses historical rates for items carried
   at historical costs and current rates to monetary current
   items.

4. In the appreciating environment, we assume that the Argentinean peso is worth more against the dollar from the beginning
of the period to the end. In the example on page 218, 60 percent of inventory is valued at the beginning of period, the rest is
valued at the end of period rate.

		Beginning of year ArP/US dollars	0.8000		
		End of year	0.9000		
		Average	0.8500		
		Inventory	0.8400		

	FASB 8	US dollars	FASB 52	US dollars
Cash and receipt net of NIBCLs	$ 50	0.9000　$ 45	0.9000	$ 45
Inventory	20	0.8400　16.8	0.9000	18
Working capital	70	62		63
Net fixed assets	930	0.8000　744	0.9000	837
	1,000	0.8058　806		700
Debt	720	0.9000　648	0.9000	648
Equity	280	0.8000　158	0.8000	224
FX gain (loss)	—	—		28
	1,000	0.8058　806		900
Revenue	2,000	0.8500　1,700	0.8500	1,700
Operating costs	(1,760)	0.8400　(1,478)	0.8500	(1,496)
SG&A	(100)	0.8500　(85)	0.8500	(85)
Depreciation	(28)	0.8000　(22)	0.8500	(24)
FX gain	—	66		—
Operating income	112	48		95
Taxes	(45)	0.8500　(38)	0.8500	(38)
NOPLAT	67	10		57
ROIC	6.73%	1.24%		6.35%
Tax rate	40.00%	79.27%		40.00%
Operating income/Sales	5.61%	2.83%		5.61%
Sales/Capital	2.00	2.11		1.89
WC/Sales	3.50%	3.64%		3.71%
NFA/Sales	46.50%	43.76%		49.24%
Operating expenses/Sales	88.00%	86.96%		88.00%
SG&A/Sales	5.00%	5.00%		5.00%
Deprecation/Sales	1.40%	1.31%		1.40%
Debt/Capital	72.00%	80.42%		72.00%
Equity/Capital	28.00%	19.58%		28.00%

The depreciating local currency shows a much different effect:

Beginning of year ArP/US dollars	0.8000
End of year	0.7000
Average	0.7500
Inventory	0.7600

	FASB 8		US dollars	FASB 52		US dollars
Cash and receipt net of NIBCLs	$ 50	0.7000	$ 35	0.7000	$ 35
Inventory	20	0.7600	15.2	0.7000	14
Working capital	70		50		49
Net fixed assets	930	0.8000	744	0.7000	651
	1,000	0.7942	794		700
Debt	720	0.7000	504	0.7000	504
Equity	280	0.8000	290	0.8000	224
FX gain (loss)	—		—		(28)
	1,000	0.7942	794		700
Revenue	2,000	0.7500	1,500	0.7500	1,500
Operating costs	(1,760)	0.7600	(1,338)	0.7500	(1,320)
SG&A	(100)	0.7500	(75)	0.7500	(75)
Depreciation	(28)	0.8000	(22)	0.7500	(21)
FX gain	—		66		—
Operating income	112		131		84
Taxes	(45)	0.7500	(34)	0.7500	(34)
NOPLAT	67		98		50
ROIC	6.73%		12.30%		7.21%
Tax rate	40.00%		25.62%		40.00%
Operating income/Sales	5.61%		8.75%		5.61%
Sales/Capital	2.00		1.89		2.14
WC/Sales	3.50%		3.35%		3.27%
NFA/Sales	46.50%		49.60%		43.40%
Operating expenses/Sales	88.00%		89.17%		88.00%
SG&A/Sales	5.00%		5.00%		5.00%
Deprecation/Sales	1.40%		1.49%		1.40%
Debt/Capital	72.00%		63.46%		72.00%
Equity/Capital	28.00%		36.54%		28.00%

FASB 52 preserves the debt-to-equity, cost structures, and tax rate, but decreases the asset-to-sales ratios. ROIC is higher than the subsidiary, but not as exaggerated as with FASB 8. The ROIC under FASB 8 results from a lower tax rate, even though efficiency and capital effective are translated in an inferior way to the original subsidiary and FASB 52's interpretation.

5. Using interest rate parity, you can invest 1 Ff at Nff and receive $(1+Nff)/X_f$. To eliminate arbitrage opportunities, this must be equal to buying Canadian dollars spot and earning $(1+Ncd)/X_0$. The forecasted forward rate in this arbitrage-free experiment is:

$$X_f = \frac{X_0\left(1+N_{cd}\right)}{\left(1+N_{ff}\right)}$$

	1	2	3	4	5	6
Cash flow (francs)	300	320	410	380	420	450
Nff (foreign)	6.9375%	8.4375%	10.3375%	11.6375%	12.8375%	13.9375%
Ncd (domestic)	7.5625%	8.6625%	9.6625%	10.7625%	11.9625%	12.9625%
$[(1+Ncd)/(1+Nff)]^t$	1.005845	1.004154	0.981759	0.969015	0.961824	0.949742
Spot rate C$/Ff	2.27	2.27	2.27	2.27	2.27	2.27
Forward rate C$/Ff.	2.283267	2.27943	2.228594	2.199665	2.183341	2.155914
Cash flow in C$	131.39	140.39	183.97	172.75	192.37	208.73
Present value at 0 in C$	644.74					

6. The parity works due to the following equivalencies:
   A. Expected change in spot rates over time equals the difference between forward and spot rates.
   B. Expected difference between inflation rates equals the expected change in spot rates.
   C. The difference in nominal interest rates equals the expected difference in inflation rates.
   D. For the same level of risk real interest rates are the same.

7. To hedge the price of acquiring NKR *1,000,000,* the factory must enter into *1,000,000* NKR/125,000 NKR/contract = *8* futures contracts. Since the factory is taking a long position, its futures prices will be the *ask* price. To see how this simple strategy locks in dollar costs, consider two scenarios: The NKR depreciates by 10 percent versus the dollar, and the NKR appreciates by 10 percent versus the dollar.

   In the first scenario, the dollar appreciates and the NKR *depreciates* to *0.65592* USD/NKR. In this case the hedged dollar costs are:

$$\text{Unhedged} - \text{Futures profit} = (\text{NKR } 1{,}000{,}000)\left(\frac{0.65592 \text{ USD}}{\text{NKR}}\right)$$
$$- 8 \text{ contracts}\left(\frac{125{,}000 \text{ NKR}}{\text{contract}}\right)\left(\frac{0.65592 \text{ USD}}{\text{NKR}} - \frac{0.7288 \text{ USD}}{\text{NKR}}\right)$$
$$= \text{USD } 728{,}800$$

   In the second case, the NKR *appreciates* while the dollar depreciates. The expected spot price will be 10 percent higher than the futures forecast on April 10, *0.80168* USD/NKR. The hedged dollar costs are:

$$\text{Unhedged} - \text{Futures profit} = (\text{NKR } 1{,}000{,}000)\left(\frac{0.80168 \text{ USD}}{\text{NKR}}\right)$$
$$- 8 \text{ contracts}\left(\frac{125{,}000 \text{ NKR}}{\text{contract}}\right)\left(\frac{0.80168 \text{ USD}}{\text{NKR}} - \frac{0.7288 \text{ USD}}{\text{NKR}}\right)$$
$$= \text{USD } 728{,}800$$

   Whether the dollar depreciates or not, the dollar cost is locked-in. The straight hedged cost is NKR *1,000,000* (*0.7288* USD/NKR) = USD *728,800.*

8. Using interest rate parity, the forward rate in 90 days (one quarter of a banker's 360 day year) is:

$$X_f = \frac{X_0\left(1 + N_d\right)}{\left(1 + N_f\right)}$$

This gives us the following table:

	NKR	USD	GBP
90-day Eurocurrency rates in following currencies	0.0575	0.06125	0.050625
Spot rates currency/USD	1.942		0.609
Forward rate/USD	1.940207		0.607407
Spot NKR/GBP	3.188834		
Forward rate NKR/GBP	3.194246		

The NKR will appreciate against the USD, while it will depreciate against GBP. The firm should go long in dollar forwards to capture the NKR appreciation against the dollar and thus minimize the number of NKRs to delivery USD 1,000,000. In making its decision to go with the U.S. gas marketer or directly with the British producer, the path that minimizes NKR outlays is with the U.S. gas marketer.

18

Valuation Outside of the United States

1. Aside from the choice of explicit forecast horizon, the ways in which value can be affected are through the estimation of NOPLAT, invested capital, net investment, and ultimately of free cash flow and economic profit. The major differences and a possible basis for comparability include:

   A. *Format* for the presentation of accounting objects.

   B. *Consolidation* of subsidiaries and minority interests. Consolidate all majority subsidiaries.

   C. *Business combinations:* Adjust for cash, stock and other means of payments, as well as the combined cost of capital relative to the riskiness of the combination.

   D. *Goodwill:* Eliminate goodwill and other intangibles from total assets. Instead, amortize against equity.

   E. *Inventory valuation methods:* Adjust to FIFO or weighted average basis. Revalue to the lower of cost or market.

   F. *Fixed asset valuation and depreciation methods:* Add back higher relative depreciation. Remove the impact of revaluation to current cost.

   G. *Discretionary reserves:* Focus on income before reserves.

H. *Income tax:* Use pretax income and use comparable marginal tax rates for each country.

I. *Foreign currency translation:* Remove foreign currency translation gains or losses.

J. *Pension accounting:* Adjust for nominal and real claims experience relative to deferred claims items.

2. The major hurdles to restatement include:
   A. Language barriers.
   B. Different meanings of accounting terms.
   C. Different reporting frequencies and auditing standards.
   D. Inadequate disclosure.

3. Here's the complete rendering:
   A. Format for the presentation of accounting objects. Notice that long term assets and liabilities are presented *first,* followed by *short term* items. Cash sales is recorded against changes in *finished goods* inventory. Either production or *cost of sales* presentations could have been made. Notes to the financial statements and a management report are *normally* required.
   B. Consolidation of subsidiaries and minority interests. Consolidation is required for parent companies that exercise control over subsidiary companies with over *50* percent of voting rights. Both *proportional* and significant control, as measured by *voting rights,* consolidations are supported.
   C. Business combinations. *Book value* and *current value* purchase methods are used.
   D. Goodwill. The goodwill amortized (*Gesamt-Abschreibungen*) is a *tax deductible* expense over a *fifteen*-year period. Goodwill is not reported under this exhibit's total assets (*Gesamtvermogen*).
   E. Inventory valuation methods. *Vorrate* is recorded at lower of *cost* or *market.* Inventory must be written down if market

values *fall below* historical cost. Inventory reserves can be used to anticipate future price changes.

F. Fixed asset valuation and depreciation methods. Straightline and declining-balance methods are the most common depreciation methods. Conservative tax tables are used to extrapolate *useful lives* for financial accounting. Thus there is practically no difference between financial and tax *depreciation,* so that deferred taxes do not normally exist. Tangibles are recorded at *historical* or *current* cost. Capital expenditures are the *net increase* in property, plant, and equipment plus *depreciation.*

G. Income tax. The commercial balance sheet determines the tax liability. Higher tax rates are applied to *fully retained* profits; a lower rate is used for *fully distributed* profits. The 50 percent tax rate is reduced by deductible municipal rates. Taxes on EBIT derive from *tax credits to shareholders,* shields on *interest* expense, tax on interest income, and *non-operating* income.

H. Foreign currency translation. A variety of translation methods are available: *temporal, closing, current,* monetary/non-monetary. Gains and losses may be transmitted either through *profit-and-loss* or *balance sheet* statements.

I. Pension accounting. *Accruals* for uncertain obligations are typically understated since they ignore accruals for *employees under 30* and they exclude future payroll increases in the actuarial *present value of future* obligations.

    Whatever the accounting standards, cash is still cash. The art is in the identification of cash items and their interpretation from diverse sources.

4. Perform the following operations with data from June 2, 2000:

A. Borrow USD 1 today and earn USD 1 + *0.076* in one year.

Borrow GBP/USD *0.66997* today and earn (GBP/USD *0.66997*)(1 + *0.065*) or *GBP 0.75352* in one year.

B. In one year GBP/USD is expected to be *0.66431.*

C. Thus, USD equivalent earned is GBP *0.75352*/GBP/USD *0.66431* or *1.074.*

D. Your conclusion about risk-free rates across heavily arbitraged currency borders is *that it does not seem to matter what risk-free rate you use for cost of capital calculations in well-arbitraged markets.*

19

Valuation in Emerging Markets

1. The effects of volatile inflation on cash flow estimation include:
    A. Assets and liabilities are recorded at historical cost and not revalued to current levels of currency units.
    B. Nominal year-to-year comparisons and ratio analysis become meaningless (e.g., ROIC and PP&E/Revenue).
    C. Continuing value cash flows require real growth and expected returns to reflect highly variable economic conditions.

2. For forecasting purposes:
    A. *Real* forecasts make it impossible to calculate taxes correctly and lead to errors in calculating working capital changes; companies grow in real terms when operating efficiencies improve.
    B. *Nominal* forecasts produce meaningless ROIC and PP&E/Revenue ratios and do not allow for realistic calculation of continuing-value cash flows; companies grow in nominal terms when, given constant real growth, inflation rises or currencies devalue.

3. The steps include:

A. Convert historical nominal balance sheets and income statements into real terms using the country's present currency value.

B. Forecast operating performance in real terms (revenues, cash expenses, working capital, property plant and equipment, and depreciation).

C. Convert operating performance items into nominal terms by multiplying the real term by the inflation index for the year. Do not adjust net PP&E, depreciation, or inventories.

D. Forecast interest expense and other non-operating income statement items in nominal terms using prior year's balance sheet.

E. Calculate income taxes based on the nominal income statement.

F. Complete the balance sheet in nominal terms by first calculating equity (last year's equity plus earnings less dividends plus/minus share issue/purchase), then balance with debt or marketable securities.

G. Complete the balance sheet in real terms by first converting debt and marketable securities with the inflation index. The equity account balances the balance sheet. To prove the sheet: Real equity should equal last year's equity, plus earnings minus dividends, plus/minus share issue/purchase, plus/minus monetary asset inflation gain/loss.

H. Calculate nominal cash flow then convert nominal to real cash flow using the inflation index.

I. Estimate continuing value using a real NOPLAT to nominal NOPLAT margin adjustment to continuing-value period NOPLAT, real reinvestment rate (real growth/real ROIC), and discounting with nominal WACC and nominal growth.

4. Here is the comparison of the various techniques:
    A. Nominal calculations:

Income, assets, cash flow	Nominal				Continuing value
	1	2	3	4	
Revenue	$1,000	$1,650	$3,086	$6,788	$8,553
EBITDA	300	495	926	2,036	2,566
Depreciation	(80)	(80)	(90)	(122)	(206)
Operating income	220	415	835	1,915	2,360
Tax	(110)	(208)	(418)	(957)	(1,180)
Net income	$ 110	$ 208	$ 418	$ 957	$1,180
Working capital	$ 200	$ 330	$ 617	$1,358	$1,711
Beginning net PPE	400	400	452	608	1,030
Less: Depreciation	(80)	(80)	(90)	(122)	(206)
Plus: Capital expenditure	80	132	247	543	684
Ending net PPE	400	452	608	1,030	1,508
Invested capital (working capital + beg PPE)	$ 600	$ 730	$1,069	$1,966	$2,740
Net income		$ 208	$ 418	$ 957	$1,180
Plus: Depreciation		80	90	122	206
Less: Working capital change		(130)	(287)	(741)	(353)
Less: Capital expenditure		(132)	(247)	(543)	(684)
Free cash flow		$ 26	$ (26)	$ (205)	$ 349

B. Deflated revenue calculation:

Income, assets, cash flow	Unadjusted real forecast				Continuing value
	1	2	3	4	
Revenue	$1,000	$1,100	$1,210	$1,331	$1,677
EBITDA	300	330	363	399	503
Depreciation	(80)	(80)	(82)	(85)	(89)
Operating income	220	250	281	315	414
Tax	(110)	(125)	(141)	(157)	(207)
Net income	$ 110	$ 125	$ 141	$ 157	$ 207
Working capital	$ 200	$ 220	$ 242	$ 266	$ 335
Beginning net PPE	400	400	408	423	445
Less: Depreciation	(80)	(80)	(82)	(85)	(89)
Plus: Capital expenditure	80	88	97	106	134
Ending net PPE	400	408	423	445	490
Invested capital (working capital + beg PPE)	$ 600	$ 620	$ 650	$ 689	$ 780
Net income		$ 125	$ 141	$ 157	$ 207
Plus: Depreciation		80	82	85	89
Less: Working capital change		(20)	(22)	(24)	(69)
Less: Capital expenditure		(88)	(97)	(106)	(134)
Free cash flow		$ 97	$ 104	$ 111	$ 93

C. Nominal translated to real calculation:

Income, assets, cash flow	Nominal to real translated				Continuing value
	1	2	3	4	
Revenue	$1,000	$1,100	$1,210	$1,331	$1,398
EBITDA	300	330	363	399	419
Depreciation	(80)	(80)	(82)	(85)	(89)
Operating income	220	250	281	315	330
Tax	(110)	(138)	(164)	(188)	(193)
Net income	$ 110	$ 112	$ 118	$ 127	$ 137
Working capital	$ 200	$ 287	$ 399	$ 544	$ 602
Beginning net PPE	400	400	408	423	445
Less: Depreciation	(80)	(80)	(82)	(85)	(89)
Plus: Capital expenditure	80	88	97	106	112
Ending net PPE	400	408	423	445	468
Invested capital (working capital + beg PPE)	$ 600	$ 687	$ 807	$ 968	$1,047
Net income		$ 112	$ 118	$ 127	$137
Plus: Depreciation		80	82	85	89
Less: Working capital change		(87)	(113)	(145)	(58)
Less: Capital expenditure		(88)	(97)	(106)	(112)
Free cash flow		$ 17	$ (10)	$ (40)	$ 57

D. Comparison:

Results: Nominal	1	2	3	4	Continuing value
Real net income	$110	$138	$164	$188	$193
Real cash flow		17	(10)	(40)	57
Beginning PPE/revenue	40%	24%	15%	9%	12%
Net income/invested capital	18%	28%	39%	49%	43%

Results	1	2	3	4	Continuing value
Real net income	$110	$125	$141	$157	$34
Real cash flow		97	104	111	15
Beginning PPE/revenue	40%	36%	34%	32%	27%
Net income/invested capital	18%	20%	22%	23%	27%

Results	Nominal to real translated				Continuing value
	1	2	3	4	
Real net income	$110	$112	$118	$127	$137
Real cash flow		17	(10)	(40)	57
Beginning PPE/revenue	40%	36%	34%	32%	32%
Net income/invested capital	18%	16%	15%	13%	13%

5. Discounted cash flow with inflation and real growth effects:

A. Nominal WACC = (1 + Real WACC) × (1 + Inflation rate) − 1
= 1.08 × 1.10 − 1 = 29.6%

B. Nominal growth rate = (1 + Real growth) × (1 + Inflation) − 1 = 1.05 × 1.20 − 1 = 26%

C. Nominal discounted cash flow:

	Nominal				Continuing value
	1	2	3	4	
Free cash flow		26	(26)	(205)	
Continuing value					9,686
Discount factor		0.6173	0.3362	0.1557	0.1557
PV of cash flow		16	(9)	(32)	1,508
DCF	1,483				
Real WACC	8.0%	8.0%	8.0%	8.0%	8.0%
Nominal WACC	29.6%	62.0%	83.6%	116.0%	29.6%
Continuing value growth					26.0%

D. Unadjusted real forecasted DCF:

	Unadjusted real forecast				Continuing value
	1	2	3	4	
Free cash flow		97	104	111	
Continuing value					3,090
Discount factor		0.9259	0.8573	0.7938	0.7938
PV of cash flow		90	89	88	2,453
DCF	2,719				
Real WACC	8.0%	8.0%	8.0%	8.0%	8.0%
Nominal WACC	Not used				
Continuing value growth					5.0%

E. Nominal to real translation DCF:

	Nominal to real translated				Continuing value
	1	2	3	4	
Free cash flow		17	(10)	(40)	
Continuing value					1,899
Discount factor		0.9259	0.8573	0.7938	0.7938
PV of cash flow		16	(9)	(32)	1,508
DCF	1,483				
Real WACC	8.0%	8.0%	8.0%	8.0%	8.0%
Nominal WACC	Not used				
Continuing value growth					5.0%

F. Real cash flows are inflated by exactly the same factor as real WACC is inflated and thus cash flow numerator and discount denominator exactly offset one another. Thus, nominal and nominal-to-real translation DCF calculation should be exactly equal if real growth rates are used in the nominal-to-real translation technique.

20

Using Option Pricing Methods to Value Flexibility

1. Here is a tool kit of risk positions:
   A. Long forward

   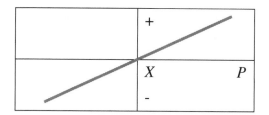

   B. Short forward

   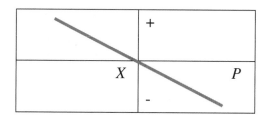

C. Long call

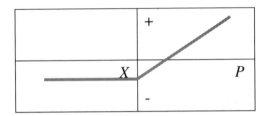

D. Short call

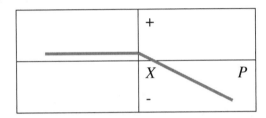

E. Long put

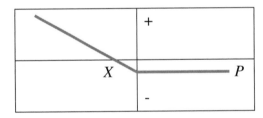

F. Short put

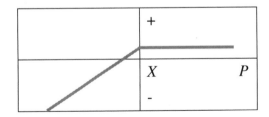

2. Let's use the toolkit to craft the new positions (dashed lines are underlying positions; solid line is resulting position):

A. *Money Spread.*

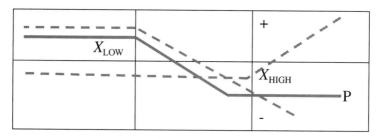

B. *Strip.*

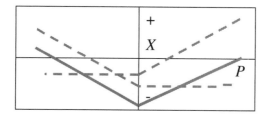

C. *Spark spread option.*

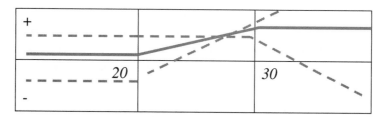

3. The expiration payoff of the put option is Max(0, $X - S$), where X is the exercise price, \$40; and S is the underlying stock price, currently at \$50. You can reproduce the put payoff by employing the following strategy:

A. Invest \$50 in the stock: long S.

B. Go long in the put by paying the put price \$3.05: long p.

C. Borrow the riskless present value of the exercise price, go short $40/(1 + 0.071/4).

r	7.1%
days	90
X	40
S	42
$X/(1+r)$	39.31
p	3.05
$S+p-X/(1+r)$	5.74

That the call price is given by $S + p - Xe^{-rt}$ can be shown using simple arbitrage principles. In 90 days, either the stock price will be greater than 40 or less than or equal to 40.

If $S > 40$, then the strategy value is:
$S + \text{Max}(0, 40 - S) - 40 = S + 0 - X = S - 40$

If $S \leq 40$, then the strategy value is:
$S + \text{Max}(0, 40 - S) - 40 = S + 40 - S - 40 = 0$

The strategy value is thus $\text{Max}(S - 40, 0)$

But this is exactly the payoff for a call option. The principle of arbitrage states that two strategies with the same payoffs will have the same value. Thus, the strategy replicates the call price. The present value of the maturity payoff strategy also replicates the present value of the call.

4. Here is one version of a possible comparison:

Input	Oil reserve	Stock option
Underlying asset value	Accumulated proven reserves discounted at convenience yield	Stock price
Exercise price	Discounted cost of developing reserve	Strike price
Time to expiration of option	Estimate of time-weighted average depletion of reserves	Maturity of option
Riskless rate	Treasury or swap rate applicable to option life	Treasury or swap rate applicable to option life
Variance in underlying asset value	Variance in oil price	Variance in stock price
Dividend yield	Convenience yield or net production revenue per reserve value	Dividend yield

5. The valuation of the mine proceeds in several movements.

    A. First, forecast the copper margin. Using the standard deviation of copper price movements, we forecast the up movement in copper margin by multiplying the previous margin by the up factor, $\exp(\sigma \Delta t)$, where σ is the annual standard deviation of copper price percent changes and Δt is the fraction or multiple of a year over which volatility endures. The downward movement in copper margin is $1/\exp(\sigma \Delta t)$ times the previous copper margin.

Riskless rate	3%	Real rate
Cu margin	0.10	Average copper margin
Sigma	20%	Standard deviation of spot copper prices
Up	1.22	Exp(Sigma × Years)
Down	0.82	1/up
Salvage/ton	0.09	Assumption

The resulting binomial tree is:

Cu Margin			
0	*1*	*2*	*3*
0.10	0.12	0.15	0.18
	0.08	0.10	0.12
		0.07	0.08
			0.05

For example, in period 1, 0.08 (downward movement from period 0) can move up to $1.22 \times 0.08 = 0.10$ or down to $0.82 \times 0.08 = 0.07$.

B. Second, forecast NOPLAT. This is the forecasted copper margin times the amount of copper mined.

Reserves	300	150	50
Mined	150	100	50

NOPLAT			
0	*1*	*2*	*3*
	18.321	14.918	9.111
	12.281	10.000	6.107
		6.703	4.094
			2.744

C. Third, we compute the straight value of the mine, that is, the value of the mine without salvage. The value of the mine at any node is the mine value expected in the next period plus the NOPLAT earned in the present node. The present value is computed based on risk neutral expectations, where, more precisely, the up branch probability is:

$$\pi = \frac{[\exp(r\,\Delta t) - \exp(-\sigma\,\Delta t)]}{[\exp(\sigma\,\Delta t) - \exp(-\sigma\,\Delta t)]}$$

This allows us to use the real portion of the riskless rate. The real portion is used because we assume that copper margins are constant inflation reflections of operations and markets.

Mine value without salvage years			
	1	2	3
30.02	36.65	22.38	9.111
	24.57	15.00	6.107
		10.06	4.094
			2.744

D. Fourth, we calculate the value of selling the mine when it becomes profitable to do so. This is dependent on the salvage value per ton remaining in the mine times the remaining reserve. The put option to sell the mine is the maximum of the value of the mine if not sold and the value if salvage or abandonment is exercised.

At the end of period 3, the value of the put option equals the Max(Margin × Remaining reserves – NOPLAT, 0). The value at nodes prior to period 3 is found in ways similar to the value of the straight mine (without salvage value). For example, after one down and one up jump in the copper margin, the value of the put option is 0.19. This is determined by finding the maximum of the intrinsic value of the option to abandon the mine versus the value to keep the mine open through period 3 (keep the salvage option alive). The formula is:

$$S(2, \text{downup}) = \text{Max} \left\{ \begin{array}{l} \text{Margin}(2, \text{downup}) \times \\ \text{Reserve}(2) - V(2, \text{downup}), \end{array} \right. $$

$$\left. \frac{\left[\begin{array}{l} [\text{Probability\_up} \times S(3, \text{downupup}) + \\ \text{Probability\_down} \times S(3, \text{downdowndown})] \end{array} \right]}{1 + r} \right\}$$

Where, S is the value of salvage and V is the value without salvage. The first term is the intrinsic value of salvage, while the second term is the value of keeping the salvage option alive. Using the data from the previous binomial trees, we have:

$$S(2, \text{downupup}) = \text{Max} \left[\frac{0.10 \times 150 - 15, \ (0.53 \times 0 + 0.47 \times 0.41)}{1.03} \right]$$

$$= 0.19$$

Similarly the value can be found for the other nodes. The year 0 node value is simply $(0.53 \times 0.09 + 0.47 \times 2.43)/1.03$, the expected present value of year 1 possible outcomes.

	Salvage value years		
	1	2	3
1.16	0.09	—	—
	2.43	0.19	—
		3.44	0.41
			1.76

The intrinsic value of the option exceeds the value of the mine with the option alive when the copper margin falls to low enough levels. This would occur when the margin is at 0.08 or lower. The firm would not wait and would exercise its option to abandon the mine at (obviously) low enough margins.

E. The total value of the mine is the value without the salvage plus the value of the salvage (abandonment) option:

Value without salvage	30.02
Salvage value	1.16
Total	31.19

21

Valuing Banks

---

1. Income using the two models:
   A. Income model:
      The income model looks like a typical income statement:

Interest income	$93.5
Interest expense	(38.0)
Other expenses	(40.0)
Net profit before tax	15.5
Taxes	(6.2)
Net income	$ 9.3

   B. The computation is simply the net interest income (income minus expense) derived from loans and deposits, minus non-interest expenses and taxes.

Loan spread	$34.0
Deposit spread	28.5
Equity credit	3.5
Reserve debit	(10.5)
Expenses	(40.0)
Net profit before tax	15.5
Taxes	(6.2)
Net income	$ 9.3

C. The two approaches are equivalent, as the numerical example shows. Here's an algebraic demonstration according to the income model:

$$NI = (r_L L - r_D D - E)\,(1-T)$$

where r_L and r_D are the loan and deposit rates, E is the non-interest expense, and T is the marginal tax rate.

For the spread model:

$$NI = \left[(r_L - r_M)L + (r_M - r_D)(D + r_M)(S - r_M)(R - E) \right](1-T)$$

where r_M = the money rate of return.

The equivalence between the two approaches can be viewed by way of the balance sheet relation:

$$R + L = D + S$$

or

$$D + S - L - R = 0$$

where R = the cash reserve
L = loans
D = deposits
S = equity

Gathering the terms in r_M in the spread model we have:

$$NI = \left[r_L L - r_D D + r_M (D + S - L - R) - E \right](1 - T)$$
$$= \left[r_L L - r_D D - E \right](1 - T)$$

just the same as the income model from the financial statements. In constructing the spread model, banks use an assumed yield, the money rate, to benchmark the profitability of loans and deposits and debit the lack of earning ability of cash reserves at the Fed. In order to square the earning abilities of various parts of the balance sheet with net income, the same rate must be used as a proxy for the cost of equity capital. The problem lies in the use of this rate to benchmark loans and deposits, and to cost the equity. Each of these items has a different risk adjusted cost of capital, and thus a different benchmark. Certainly the money rate is not at all necessarily related to the equity cost of capital and can be reliably assigned only to the cash reserve account. Allocations based on the spread model must be viewed with caution since they do not represent comparisons of investments (short and long) with their risk-adjusted opportunity costs of capital.

2. Develop a narrative account to forecast a bank's balance sheet and income statement:

The model starts with a forecast of *deposit* growth. Loans are then determined by a *loan to total deposit* ratio. *Cash* reserves work from a cash reserve-to-total deposit ratio, reflecting Federal Reserve policy. Premises, equipment and other assets are required to support deposits directly and loans indirectly. Investments are related to cash reserves. Given a level of *deposit derived total assets,* a managerially determined *liability* to total asset relationship is determined. Federal Funds Purchased balances *liabilities. Equity* balances the balance sheet. Non-interest income and expense are related to deposit size. Forecasts of interest rates drive the *deposit,* term borrowing, investment, and *loan* rates.

3. The valuation moves in several steps:

   A. First, a set of assumptions:

Neighborhood Banking System, Inc.
Key ratios and assumptions

	Historical	Explicit forecast period			CV period
	1999	2000	2001	2002	2003
Loan/deposit	68.48%	72.00%	71.00%	70.00%	69.00%
Other liabilities/ total assets	0.70%	0.70%	0.70%	0.70%	0.70%
Term borrowing/ total assets	12.04%	12.00%	12.00%	12.00%	12.00%
Liabilities/total assets	93.62%	94.00%	94.00%	94.00%	93.00%
Cash reserves/investment	8.56%	8.50%	8.50%	8.50%	8.50%
Cash reserves/deposits	4.97%	5.00%	5.00%	5.00%	5.00%
Deposit growth	15.00%	15.00%	12.00%	10.00%	0.00%
Provision for loan loss/ net loans	1.41%	1.40%	1.40%	1.40%	1.40%
Premises, other assets/ deposits	3.92%	3.92%	3.92%	3.92%	3.92%
Other income/deposits	0.79%	0.75%	0.75%	0.75%	0.75%
Other expenses/deposits	4.07%	4.10%	4.10%	4.10%	4.10%
Depreciation/net premises	5.62%	5.62%	5.62%	5.62%	5.62%
Beta	1.20	1.30	1.40	1.40	1.30

   B. Next, the income statement shown on page 248.

   C. Now the balance sheet shown on page 249.

Income statement

| | Explicit forecast period | | | | | | | | CV period | |
| | 1999 | | 2000 | | 2001 | | 2002 | | 2003 | |
	Amount	Rate	Amount	Rate	Amount	Rate	Amount	Rate	Amount	Rate
Interest income	66.919	8.11%	87.087	8.89%	104.880	9.63%	123.306	10.37%	83.527	7.08%
Interest expense	(25.221)	3.52%	(33.501)	3.91%	(45.286)	4.76%	(58.346)	5.62%	(46.686)	4.59%
Net interest income	41.698	4.59%	53.587	4.97%	59.594	4.87%	64.960	4.75%	36.841	2.49%
Other income	5.120		5.619		6.293		6.923		6.923	
Other expenses	(26.498)		(30.717)		(34.403)		(37.844)		(37.844)	
Net profit before tax	20.320		82.075		91.077		98.999		42.761	
Taxes	(7.721)	38.00%	(31.188)	38.00%	(34.609)	38.00%	(37.620)	38.00%	(16.249)	38.00%
Net income	12.598		50.886		56.468		61.379		26.512	

Balance sheet

	1999		Explicit forecast period				CV period			
			2000		2001		2002		2003	
	Amount	Rate	Amount	Rate	Amount	Rate	Amount	Rate	Amount	Rate
Cash reserves	32.411		37.460		41.955		46.151		46.151	
Investment securities	378.520	6.93%	440.706	7.68%	493.591	8.43%	542.950	9.18%	542.950	6.00%
Net loans	446.135	9.12%	539.425	9.87%	595.765	10.62%	646.111	11.37%	636.881	8.00%
Net premises, other assets	25.526		29.369		32.893		36.182		36.182	
Less: Provision for credit losses	(6.281)		(7.552)		(8.341)		(9.046)		(8.916)	
Total assets	876.311		1,039.408		1,155.863		1,262.349		1,253.248	
Interest bearing deposits	552.892	3.29%	635.826	4.29%	712.125	5.29%	783.337	6.29%	783.337	5.00%
Non-interest bearing deposits	98.587		113.375		126.980		139.678		139.678	
Other short term liabilities	6.102		7.276		8.091		8.836		8.773	
Federal funds purchased	57.300	4.00%	95.838		100.612		103.274		83.342	
Term borrowings	105.550	4.49%	124.729	4.99%	138.704	5.49%	151.482	5.99%	150.390	5.00%
Liabilities	820.431		977.043		1,086.511		1,186.608		1,165.520	
Shareholders' equity	55.880	13.48%	62.364	14.02%	69.352	14.56%	75.741	14.56%	87.727	14.02%
Total	876.311		1,039.408		1,155.863		1,262.349		1,253.248	

D. Finally, equity cash flows and the value to the equity holders:

Equity cash flow and value		Explicit forecast period			CV period
	1999	2000	2001	2002	2003
Net income		50.886	56.468	61.379	26.512
Depreciation		1.651	1.849	2.033	2.033
Less: Increase in assets		(163.097)	(116.455)	(106.485)	9.101
Plus: Increase in liabilities		156.612	109.468	100.096	(21.087)
Equity cash flow		46.052	51.329	57.024	16.559
Present value factor		0.8770391	0.7655719	0.6682715	
PV equity cash flows		40.390	39.296	38.107	
PV continuing value				78.929	
Market value of equity	196.723				
Number of shares	5.987				
Stock price	32.86				

22

Valuing Insurance Companies

---

1. Outline the steps needed to value an insurance company:
   A. study historical perfomance
   B. forecast future cash flow, cost of capital and economic profit
   C. estimate continuing value
   D. estimate equity value

2. Summarize Transamerica's historical experience:
   A. Revenue developments: premiums are volatile; investment income return is declining in the bull market although investment income is rising secularly.
   B. Expense developments: other expense continues to exceed other revenue.
   C. Free cash flow experience: cash flow is volatile during period of premium decline but claims increase.
   D. Benefits versus premium: benefits and claims exceed premiums, but premium grow faster than claims. Investment income pays for benefits while premiums accrete assets for investment against reserves.

3. Characterize an alternative scenario for Transamerica using the following drivers for years 1999–2001 and separately in perpetuity:

    A. Net premium growth: grow net premiums using innovative programs for life, property and casualty to 3% and declining to long-term growth of 2%.

    B. Investment income rate: deploy portfolio risk management and transaction engineering techniques to more cost effectively hedge volatile investments while placing secure return floor.

4. Forecasts of income statement, balance sheet, cash flow and economic profit statements follow:

Income statement ($ million)	1999	2000	2001	2002	CV
Net premium income	1,902	1,969	2,028	2,079	2,120
Interest income (investments)	2,405	2,422	2,439	2,293	2,310
Realized capital gains	32	32	33	33	33
Interest income (loans)	747	792	840	890	943
Other revenues	1,266	1,291	1,317	1,343	1,370
Total revenues	6,353	6,506	6,656	6,638	6,777
Benefits and claims	(2,949)	(3,013)	(3,103)	(3,181)	(3,244)
Amortization of acquisition costs	(278)	(287)	(296)	(303)	(310)
Other expense	(1,823)	(1,808)	(1,844)	(1,881)	(1,918)
Total operating expenses	(5,049)	(5,108)	(5,243)	(5,365)	(5,472)
Interest expense	(533)	(466)	(508)	(550)	(592)
Income before exceptional provisions	771	933	906	723	714
Exceptional provisions	—	—	—	—	—
Income before taxes	771	933	906	723	714
Income taxes	(270)	(327)	(317)	(253)	(250)
Income before extraordinary items	501	606	589	470	464
Extraordinary items	—	—	—	—	—
Net income	501	606	589	470	464

Income statement ($ million)	1999	2000	2001	2002	CV
Beginning retained earnings	3,746	3,753	3,760	3,767	3,774
Net income	501	606	589	470	464
Common dividends	(175)	(212)	(206)	(165)	(162)
Preferred dividends	—	—	—	—	—
Potential dividends	(319)	(387)	(376)	(299)	(295)
Adjustments	—	—	—	—	—
Ending retained earnings	3,753	3,760	3,767	3,774	3,781

Notes:

- Net income lines are estimated by straight-forward multiplication of ratios times quantities.
- Investment income depends on balance sheet forecasts below.
- Potential dividends derive from cash flow statement forecasts below. These are equity cash flows in excess of the scheduled dividend to common shareholders.

Balance sheet ($ million)	1999	2000	2001	2002	CV
Assets					
Insurance investments	32,067	32,291	32,523	32,761	33,006
Cash and short term investments	127	130	133	133	136
Excess marketable securities	—	—	—	—	—
Accounts receivable	2,230	2,308	2,377	2,437	2,485
Net tangible fixed assets	3,488	3,572	3,654	3,644	3,721
Intangible assets	423	423	423	423	423
Deferred policy acquisition costs	2,144	2,219	2,286	2,343	2,390
Separate account assets	9,829	10,615	11,465	12,382	13,372
Other assets	7,866	8,338	8,839	9,369	9,931
Total assets	58,174	59,897	61,699	63,491	65,463

Balance sheet ($ million)	1999	2000	2001	2002	CV
Liabilities and shareholders' equity					
Total debt	8,200	8,200	8,200	8,200	8,200
Accounts payable	2,363	2,420	2,476	2,469	2,521
Separate account liabilities	9,829	10,615	11,465	12,382	13,372
New debt	(1,034)	(388)	268	902	1,578
Total liabilities	19,358	20,848	22,409	23,954	25,672
Provisions and reserves	32,388	32,614	32,848	33,089	33,336
Minority interest	715	715	715	715	715
Preferred shares	—	—	—	—	—
Common shares	70	70	70	70	70
Share premium	—	—	—	—	—
Net unrealized capital gains	1,943	1,943	1,943	1,943	1,943
Retained earnings	3,746	3,753	3,760	3,767	3,774
Transfers and other movements	(46)	(46)	(46)	(46)	(46)
Total shareholders' equity	5,713	5,720	5,727	5,734	5,741
Total liabilities and shareholders' equity	58,174	59,897	61,699	63,491	65,463
Beginning provisions and reserves	32,388	32,614	32,848	33,089	33,336
Increase in reserves	209	217	223	229	233
Increase in provisions	17	17	18	18	19
Ending provisions and reserves	32,614	32,848	33,089	33,336	33,588

Notes:
- First estimate provisions and reserves using ratios for increase in reserves and provisions.
- Then use estimated provisions and reserves to estimate investments
- The line of forecast moves from premium forecast to provisions and reserves to investment and back to investment income on the income statement.
- Estimate the rest of the assets using ratios and growth assumptions.

- Estimate accounts payable. Separate account liabilities exactly offset separate account assets.
- Net realized capital gains are assumed to be 1.943 across all forecast periods.
- Insert retained earnings from the income statement.
- Calculate New debt as the residual between (Total assets) and (Shareholders' equity plus Total debt plus Accounts payable plus Separate account liabilities plus Provisions and reserves, Common shares, Net unrealized capital gains, Transfers).

Cash flow statement ($ million)	1999	2000	2001	2002	CV
Net premium income	1,902	1,969	2,028	2,079	2,120
Amortization of deferred acquisition costs	(278)	(287)	(296)	(303)	(310)
Insurance profit before benefits and claims	1,625	1,682	1,732	1,775	1,811
	—	226.01	233.92	240.93	246.96
Benefits and claims	(2,949)	(3,013)	(3,103)	(3,181)	(3,244)
Increase in insurance liabilities and reserves	—	226	234	241	247
Net cash benefits and claims paid	(2,949)	(2,787)	(2,869)	(2,940)	(2,997)
Net insurance cash flow	(1,324)	(1,105)	(1,137)	(1,164)	(1,186)
Net interest income	2,405	2,422	2,439	2,293	2,310
Other income	2,013	2,083	2,157	2,233	2,314
Other expense	(1,823)	(1,808)	(1,844)	(1,881)	(1,918)
Exceptional income and provisions	—	—	—	—	—
Income taxes	(270)	(327)	(317)	(253)	(250)
Realized capital gains	32	32	33	33	33
Extraordinary items	—	—	—	—	—
Cash from operations	1,034	1,298	1,330	1,261	1,303
Other cash sources					
Increase in accounts payable and other liabilities	(31)	57	56	(7)	52
Total other cash sources	(31)	57	56	(7)	52

(continued)

Cash flow statement ($ million)	1999	2000	2001	2002	CV
Cash uses					
Increase in investments	(1,589)	224	232	239	245
Increase in cash and short-term investments	(32)	3	3	(0)	3
Increase in accounts receivable	(24)	78	69	59	49
Increase in fixed assets	(39)	84	82	(10)	76
Increase in intangible and other assets	579	472	500	530	562
Increase in deferred acquisition costs	49	75	67	57	47
Total cash uses	(1,056)	936	953	875	981
Cash flow before financing	2,059	419	433	380	373
Increase in debt	(1,032)	646	656	634	676
Minority interest	—	—	—	—	—
Increase in preferred stock	—	—	—	—	—
Interest expense	(533)	(466)	(508)	(550)	(592)
Equity cash flow	494	599	582	463	457
Dividends	175	212	206	165	162
Potential dividends	319	387	376	299	295
Increase in common stock and adjustments to retained earnings	—	—	—	—	—
Equity cash flow	494	599	582	463	457

Notes:

- Drop income statement forecasts into the cash flow forecast.
- Calculate changes in balance sheet items.
- Potential dividends equal pre-common share dividend equity cash flow minus the common share dividend.

Economic profit statement ($ million)	1999	2000	2001	2002	CV
Economic profit					
Beginning equity	5,706	5,713	5,720	5,727	5,734
Return on beginning equity	8.8%	10.6%	10.3%	8.2%	8.1%
Cost of equity	9.4%	9.4%	9.4%	9.4%	9.4%
Spread	−0.6%	1.2%	0.9%	−1.2%	−1.3%
Economic profit	(36)	69	51	(68)	(75)
Economic profit (adjust for unrealized cap gains)					
Beginning equity (less unrealized capital gains)	3,763	3,770	3,777	3,784	3,791
Return on beginning equity	13.3%	16.1%	15.6%	12.4%	12.2%
Cost of equity	9.4%	9.4%	9.4%	9.4%	9.4%
Spread	3.9%	6.7%	6.2%	3.0%	2.8%
Economic profit	147	252	234	114	108

Notes:

- Cost of equity is already forecast in Chapter 22 of the book.
- Equity cash flows do not adjust for unrealized capital gains.
- Economic profit is beginning equity times the spread between equity return and cost of capital.

5. Continuing value is calculated as follows:
   A. Cash flow: CV net income/Equity cost of capital in perpetu-
      ity = 464/0.094 = 4,936; zero growth, whatever the rein-
      vestment rate.
   B. Economic profit: CV economic profit/Equity cost of capital =
      108/0.094 = 1,135.

6. Here is the equity estimate

$ million	1999	2000	2001	2002	CV
Cash flow	494	599	582	463	4,936
Economic profit adjusted for					
unrealized gains	147	252	234	114	1,145
PV factor	0.9141	0.8355	0.7637	0.6981	0.6381
PV of CF	451	501	444	323	3,446
PV of EP	134	211	178	80	799

$ million	DCF	EP
Operating value	5,165	1,402
Beginning equity (less		
unrealized gains)		3,763
Equity value	5,165	5,165
Plus: unrealized gains	1,943	1,943
Estimated equity value	7,108	7,108
Market value of equity	7,045	7,045
Percent difference between		
market and estimate	0.9%	0.9%